BNP

OTHER EDITIONS IN THIS SERIES

George Garrett, guest editor, *Best New Poets 2005*

Eric Pankey, guest editor, *Best New Poets 2006*

Natasha Trethewey, guest editor, *Best New Poets 2007*

Mark Strand, guest editor, *Best New Poets 2008*

Kim Addonizio, guest editor, *Best New Poets 2009*

Claudia Emerson, guest editor, *Best New Poets 2010*

D.A. Powell, guest editor, *Best New Poets 2011*

Matthew Dickman, guest editor, *Best New Poets 2012*

Brenda Shaughnessy, guest editor, *Best New Poets 2013*

Dorianne Laux, guest editor, *Best New Poets 2014*

Tracy K. Smith, guest editor, *Best New Poets 2015*

Mary Szybist, guest editor, *Best New Poets 2016*

Best
NEW
Poets

2017

50 Poems from Emerging Writers

Guest Editor Natalie Diaz

Series Editor Jeb Livingood

This book was published in cooperation with *Meridian* (readmeridian.org) and the University of Virginia Press (upress.virginia.edu).

For additional information, visit us at
bestnewpoets.org
twitter.com/BestNewPoets
facebook.com/BestNewPoets

Cover and interior design elements originally by Atomicdust | atomicdust.com

Text set in Adobe Garamond Pro and Bodoni

Printed by Thomson-Shore, Dexter, Michigan

ISBN: 978-0997562316
ISSN: 1554-7019

Contents

About *Best New Poets*

Welcome to *Best New Poets 2017*, our thirteenth annual anthology of fifty poems from emerging writers. In *Best New Poets*, the term "emerging writer" is defined narrowly: we restrict our anthology to poets who have yet to publish a book-length collection of poetry. Our goal is to provide special encouragement and recognition to poets just starting in their careers, the many writing programs they attend, and the magazines that publish their work.

From February to May of 2017, *Best New Poets* accepted nominations from writing programs and magazines in the United States and Canada. Each magazine and program could nominate two writers, and those poets could send a free submission to the anthology. For a small entry fee, writers who had not received nominations could also submit poems as part of our open competition. Eligible poems were either published after January 1, 2016, or unpublished. Which means you are not only reading new poets in this book, but also some of their most recent work.

In all, we received over 2,000 submissions for a total of roughly 3,750 poems. A pool of readers and the series editor ranked these submissions, sending a few hundred selections to this year's guest editor, Natalie Diaz, who chose the final fifty poems that appear here.

Kai Carlson-Wee
Rail

I find it here in the wild alfalfa, head full
of anti-psychotics and blue rain. Twenty years old
on a freight train riding the soy fields
into the night. Leaning away from the shortgrass
prairie, the black Mississippi of dream.
My brother asleep on the well-wall beside me,
nodding his head to the sway. What home
are we leaving? What distances blur
the electric fence? What hundred low thundering
wheels of darkness are coming to carry us
there? Rain and the singing wind, over
the auto-racks. Staring out west at the stars
of our gods and the lonely dark stars of our hearts.
Boarded-up store fronts, burned down
apartments, highway signs that only name
the dead. We cross the station tracks,
the broken legs of Sunday chairs left rusting
in the yards. We know the way the story ends.
Still, the whistle blows. The flare-stacks whip
their excess methane candles against
the night. The wheels that brought us this far
still roll, still churn the polished iron ash.
The road goes on. The highway turns a deeper
shade of black. And as the sun sinks down
on the eastern Montana hills, peppered with horses
and gun-shot cars, the rails still lead us
somewhere else, and shine in the falling light.

—Nominated by *New England Review*

Jameson Fitzpatrick
I Woke Up

and it was political.
I made coffee and the coffee was political.
I took a shower and the water was.
I walked down the street in short shorts and a Bob Mizer tank top
and they were political, the walking and the shorts and the beefcake
silkscreen of the man posing in a G-string. I forgot my sunglasses
and later, on the train, that was political,
when I studied every handsome man in the car.
Who I thought was handsome was political.
I went to work at the university and everything was
very obviously political, the department and the institution.
All the cigarettes I smoked between classes were political,
where I threw them when I was through.
I was blond and it was political.
So was the difference between "blond" and "blonde."
I had long hair and it was political. I shaved my head and it was.
That I didn't know how to grieve when another person was killed in America
was political, and it was political when America killed another person,
who they were and what color and gender and who I am in relation.
I couldn't think about it for too long without feeling a helplessness
like childhood. I was a child and it was political, being a boy
who was bad at it. I couldn't catch and so the ball became political.
My mother read to me almost every night
and the conditions that enabled her to do so were political.
That my father's money was new was political, that it was proving something.
Someone called me faggot and it was political.
I called myself a faggot and it was political.
How difficult my life felt relative to how difficult it was

was political. I thought I could become a writer
and it was political that I could imagine it.
I thought I was not a political poet and still
my imagination was political.
It had been, this whole time I was asleep.

—Nominated by *Poetry*

Samantha Grenrock
It Is Known to the State of California

This jetway puts you at risk
for a host of maladies, for instance, cancer,
black lung, birth defects,
            depression, just

standing here watching time eat itself
like a snake. Among other things,
traveling by air, you are exposed to millions of particles.
            Possibly soot. Dust

off the continent. Dark matter, for instance.
It is known to the state of California
that down in the desert, on a stretch of road
            without mile-markers

or a Joshua tree to throw down the hour, radio waves leap
into the great day-moon emptiness, where the skies
ache with swallows whose mud-and-straw roosts
in the eaves of the old mission

built by natives who found God on their knees
have been demolished. They have taken up with the crows,
who by the thousands can be seen each evening flocking
            to the brutalist arcades

of the community college. It is known that migratory patterns
are subject to change. The monarch sans milkweed
navigates the freeways by smell alone for her two-week lifespan,
　　　　kissing the concrete's garland

of graffiti, meaningless, but for what was risked
jumping chain link and razor wire with a can of bubblegum script.
It is known to the state of California that the coyote
　　　　trotting through the subdivision

doesn't leave scat or tracks, for everyone sees it plain as day
in the daylight. It is known to the coyote that all land is his land now,
including the cats, the small dogs left out back.
　　　　Same goes for the brown bears

dumpster diving miles outside their natural habitat.
It is known to the state of California that the hills are burning
up to the very edge, and it takes a gallon of water to birth
　　　　a handful of peaches.

Be fruitful and multiply was a loose translation.
Now we can't take any more people in our boat,
and the Donners are still eating ox hide and each other in the endless snows
　　　　of westward, westward.

Vanessa Moody
Anniversary III

1.

Hi Vanessa

I received the MRI report of your MRI and MRA scan done yesterday.
The residual trigeminal mass lesion is 3.2 x 2.9 x 1.9 cm in size. The
MRA of the blood vessels showed normal carotid artery—no vascular
compression. If they gave you a copy of the images, we can look at it.
I suggest you have a follow up surgical consultation, either at the -----
Medical Center, or with the surgeons who previously operated on you.

I hope the Trileptal is helping with the trigeminal neuralgia pain.

2.

Hi Vanessa

yesterday
the lesion showed
no you

a copy
look at it

you or
who

you

the pain.

3.

I report and scan.
Done!

The mass size.
The blood.

Look:
You, I hope.

4.

Vanessa.

report your yesterday
residual blood

look at it.

follow
operate

on the helping
the pain

5.

I   your

                                                they   you
we   it. I
          you
                who   you.

I hope   pain.

6.

done size up the surgeons
(surgical surgeons)

done copy the look
(suggest hope)

done blood the images
(medical pain)

7.

I received your mass
gave you the images

we can look up
at the ----- with you

8.

I suggest you have a follow up

I suggest you have a follow up
I suggest you have a follow up
I suggest you have a follow up
surgical consultation
I suggest you have a follow up
I suggest you have a follow up
surgical consultation

I suggest you have a follow up
surgical consultation

I suggest you have a follow up
I suggest consultation

I suggest a follow up consultation

I suggest you have a follow up
I suggest you have a follow up
I suggest you have a follow up
surgical consultation

I have
have you
you follow
follow up
up surgical
surgical surgical
suggest you
have you

surgical
surgical

Vanessa

9.

3.2 x 2.9 x 1.9

10.

Vanessa of the mass-is-normal
you of the images

we can.

(you have a center)

you is.

Chad Abushanab
On the Dred Ranch Road Just off 283

Stars are fired up like scattershot.
The howls of wolves who saunter near extinction
carry across the plains until they're not.
All of them are headed one direction.

My father was a drinker. So am I—
an echo of a tune in drunken time.
The bottle is an instrument, and rye
the amber music spilling over. I'm

thinking about the rhythm of decline:
he measured his in knuckles, hookers, drinks.
I start to wonder how I'll measure mine,
the ballad of the triple-whisky jinx,

but the wind begins to sigh, a tired thing.
I pull the bottle from the bag. It sings.

Paige Lewis
The Moment I Saw a Pelican Devour

a seagull—wings swallowing wings—I learned
that a miracle is anything that God forgot
to forbid. So when you tell me that saints

are splintered into bone bits smaller than
the freckles on your wrist and that each speck
is sold to the rich, I know to marvel at this

and not the fact that these same saints are still
wholly intact and fresh-faced in their Plexiglas
tomb displays. We holy our own fragments

when we can—trepanation patients wear their
skull spirals as amulets, mothers frame the dried
foreskin of their firstborn, and I've seen you

swirl my name on your tongue like a thirst pebble.
Still, I try to hold on to nothing for fear of being
crushed by what can be taken because sometimes

not even our mouths belong to us. Listen, in
the early 1920s, women were paid to paint radium
onto watch dials so that men wouldn't have to ask

the time in dark alleys. They were told it was safe,
told to lick their brushes into sharp points. These
women painted their nails, their faces, and judged

whose skin shined brightest. They coated their
teeth so their boyfriends could see their bites
with the lights turned down. The miracle here

is not that these women swallowed light. It's that,
when their skin dissolved and their jaws fell off,
the Radium Corporation claimed they all died

from syphilis. It's that you're telling me about
the dull slivers of dead saints, while these
women are glowing beneath our feet.

Connor Yeck
Nevada

he stood at the mark of the forty-acre
gate, hacking sage, oiling the gun-
flat piston of the hinge

when he saw them coming down;
not out of the sky, but over it—
a shoal of horses lost

in their talk of dust.

they came to drink at the creek-head
a half-mile off, parting the high
hillside, its burnways
of daylight

& cloud-caldera.

at times, he turned to watch them; halted
his prying at the broke jaw of the gate-
post; as he ate his cold lunch

in the cabin of the truck; & when finished
for the day, lingered.

at the creek-shore, the cottonwoods
were coughing their tufts, seed-
work like blanks, tamped
on the water—

& it was there he saw the horses
had no eyes.

& how to have no eyes as a horse
seemed the act of a temple
judge, something so
just in its own
clarity,

a thing out of greater time.

he had seen other animals of course,
wandered from the testing site.
a hare, once, a bighorn—

burnt angles of the curling cornice-
horn bent by distant masons.

& he saw now how the horses
were dunking their heads
into the water, again &
again, & he saw

how their skins were shone away,
pink & white & cream & black—
necks stretched in the cinch

of living leather.

Kien Lam
Ode to Working

at Taco Bell
with your mother
who is called Mom
by all your coworkers
so you wonder
if you should call her
something else
to make them think
you have that special
mother-son bond
you see on the *Discovery*
Channel when blue
whales offer a hundred
gallons of milk
each day to their offspring
and show them
the migratory routes
coded into their DNA,
which is not too different
from your mother
sliding you a little extra food
when you take your break.
Family legends say
you were born there,
straight out of a bag of ground
beef in spite of regulations,
and the meat, if you
can call it that, tasted

fine, and in spite
of the strict codes
your boss maintains,
the plastic
bag of meat still looks
like a plastic bag of meat,
which is to say it
looks like it just crawled
out of some creature's
womb, which is why you lie
in bed sometimes
in the middle of night
when your stomach growls
for a third meal and think
about all the nasty shit
that must be part of your
genetic composition—the cattle
flesh minced and salvaged, picked
clean off the bone, the mystery
chemicals a mixture of sweat
and blood, all the stupid
things you've placed into your
mouth, all the times
you said Mom and she turned
her head to look at you
and see what you wanted.

—Nominated by *Southern Indiana Review*

Christina Im
Meanwhile in America

My mother has a dream in August and won't tell me
how it ends. On the fence the crow counts to ten.
In a month we will all be citizens and the man
on the radio knows it. Limns us into nightmare:

imaginary capital thrown to the page. Red as a shock
to the tongue. And all the lights nothing more
than ways to fill containers. *What kind of language
lets that happen?* I don't know—

is what I want to say but can't. I hear it all.
This can be wire and warp. This can be a story
that forgets to move like a story. This can be told
and retold—every time in the wrong country. I'll wait.

*

Act of creation: I dissolve
out of the dark. Yellow,

by which I mean white
but cheaper. I stand only to warn

and be warned. Keep still. Today
I am the body politic. Today I am

the body.

*

My eyes are dry for three years. At breakfast
my mother tells me five times to be safe. She remembers
how gently the stray grenade slips out of a hand, into
a family tree. How gently the hand

slips out of the girl, into its own pale orbit. Nothing
is wasted. Nothing is better than this. I'm trying to be
specific. On television we are all of us thieves. Or better,
the reason the sky looks so much closer than it did

yesterday. The dawn breaks on my knee, acrid
and faithless: proof that I come from somewhere.
It's always been too late. Wednesday. Smoke-
screen. The crow at the window watches us eat.

*

Act of creation: the radio
on my desk—the dial murmurs

away from my touch.
My ancestors flicker out

of its jaw, curving smooth as an order
to kill. The bulb above my head spitting

in my mother tongue.

*

Autumn now. Dislocated into any other hour,
I'd warpath my face bright with tar. The rain sours.
It's breaking records this year. Like everything else
I've ever touched. Get your gas masks right here—

quick, while they're still selling them to you. Quick,
while words are still words and they still fit between
your mother's bones. Along the highway the billboards,
unblinking. I'm speeding. Thinking I could build a house

with all those weapons. But the man on the poster,
the intercom, the history book, fixed on the distance
from my hips to my chest, holds me down when I cry
fire! in the theater. *Progress,* he says. *Look at you, all safe.*

                *

Act of creation: turn it off.
Turn it all off. Yellow,

by which I mean too hollowed-
out even for the birds, by which

I mean starving slowly
to life. The radio man,

he sees us. He is so afraid.

                *

I will say this: it's nice being talked about.
Too weak to stay. Too good to live. Incandescent
at the prophet's feet. Crow's wings aflame
behind the metal curtain between my legs.

This was going to be about my mother. This is
still about my mother. Don't you know
these are dangerous times we die in?
Minor chord, first inversion—

foreign girl found splayed in the prophet's
backseat. The woman who raised her, shuddering
back into color. No sound. I will say this: it's nice
knowing what I know about tyrants.

*

Act of creation: a world,
unarmed. Three times,

check the locks.

*

Sometimes I picture the house, after. The land
laughing on its axis precisely because
it shouldn't be. I can't decide whether I've made it
this far. Can't decide how to decide. Anyway,

no human could breathe this fog. Not without
someplace to return to. Mother, I miss you. Next time
I want to be smarter. As if that will get me out.
I want a storyteller here at all times. Look at me,

still so helpful. Next time the crows
could sing a song of sickness: these vowels
are murder on the heart, mother. They slacken
in the throat like dust.

Anna Newman
Fairy Tale with the Silver Gun

I

I was trying to get rid of the gun before I got rid of myself. The gun was my father's, meant for hunting, but I held it in my hands like it was a spoon I could nestle in the back of my throat. This was the time of the deer-cull. Out in the forest behind our house other hunters took down deer with brittle snapping sounds while their dogs arched and leapt through the ivy like silver fish flipping in the air at the fish run. The deer felt the bullets nip at their heels like cold air. Fear licked at them like a red tongue. My greyhound nosed open the glass door of our house and ran out, sturdy and straight as a minnow. I shot the gun into the air to call him back, because its voice was louder than mine, and because my hand wanted to hold that trigger so badly. Right before the bullet hit him my dog's mouth stretched over the head of a white rabbit like a magician's hat.

II

The colors were a tapestry on the floor of a castle in a children's book: the blood almost purple, like a king's cloak. The ivy in the winter, curled around his bones, looked like foam lapping up around a pile of shells. Or eels gathered around stones. A picture on the wall of the deer-cull that year: my father smiling, mounted antlers behind his back like brown wings. The hide stretched taut on the wall like a moth. Everything transforming into something else, except for me: sitting there in the glass-walled room that was my childhood. At night, in sleep, my hand rested naturally against my throat in the shape of a gun, barrel pressing up. If this were a fairy-tale, the gun would suck back the night of his death like a ghost into its barrel. But I was still holding the gun months later. My heart still waiting to be swept from its chimney.

—Nominated by the University of Maryland
MFA Program

Alyssa Ogi
Tree Haibun

A teacher says my poetry is too preoccupied with race. There is nothing timeless about sensationalism, and he quotes Coleridge as if Coleridge parroted the words of God. He tells me to examine pine trees for wisdom. In this institution, I am expected to be the best, expected to be obedient enough to excel, and excel I do. At everything, at once, not only on paper, but in the stall of a library toilet, where I throw up the words I've swallowed down all day. The burn feels natural, as if my great-great-grandmothers taught me how to purge in a dream. No one said that it'd feel cathartic; that the damage might be intentional. I'm preoccupied with my skin color in the light, and the weight of excellence around my belly. So yes, profess admiration that I can be the opposite of dangerous and the opposite of safe at once. Profess that a man snuck a hand up a modest skirt hem on a Los Angeles bus and I couldn't stop him, crushed by other passengers. I don't know what he looked like, though his cologne smelled like pine trees. I don't know why a man stopped my lover and me once, as we exited the Chandler Pavilion in our nicest clothes. Salieri's *The Great Kubla Khan of the Tartars* premiered; actors taped back their eyelids. We left early to catch our bed. The strange man had dimples like mine and asked where he could buy a girl like me in the city. No one knew where that question was directed: at a blond-haired American, at a black-haired American, at a preoccupied laugh track long since discarded. Two men laughed and one woman draped a sweater over her obedient dress, with beadwork that resembled trees across its hem. On the walk toward our metro line, love reached for me. Love told me that some people liked to get a rise out of others. I named the insult *sensational,* but it came out as *timeless.* Love reached for me and said I was overreacting, so I did what I do best.

*

Pine bends in snowstorms
until it breaks in the summer,
ill-prepared for warmth.

Edgar Kunz

Free Armchair, Worcester

He pinches the j between his first two fingers squints an eye against the ribbon of smoke sliding up and over his cheekbone. It's me my buddy Ant and Ant's step-dad Randy a half-ass house painter who's always trying to hit us up for weed or pills even though we're thirteen and don't do pills or have any idea how to get them. We're driving Randy's work van into Worcester to pick up a recliner he found in the free section of the Globe. Ant hates his guts and I don't like him much either but Ant's always doing stuff for me like asking his mom if I can stay the night when I get kicked out or sneaking me empanadas when my dad doesn't come home so I go along Ant up front me in the back bracing myself against the wheel wells trying not to get knocked around too bad. Randy pulls up in front of the house and we try stuffing the armchair in the back but the arms are too wide. We flip it on one end heave it onto the roof lash it down with a tangle of rope from the glovebox step back. It's not a bad looking chair. Fabric ratty at the edges but sturdy. Mostly clean. Randy twists another j to celebrate and buys us sandwiches. We post up in an Arby's parking lot the three of us cracking jokes Randy belting folk songs in Spanish. Recliner strapped to the van like a prize buck. He flicks the roach into the weeds says but you skinny-asses you little faggots you could barely lift it and we stop laughing. I look over at Ant and he's sort of picking at his jeans face tight like he got caught doing something dumb like he's ashamed or something and for a second it's like what's gonna happen has already happened. Like the rope's already snapped the armchair gone headlong into the road behind us. Like we're pulled off on the shoulder Randy punching the wheel calling us dumbfucks fuckheads sons-of-bitches. Sending us out to wait for a lull in traffic drag the wreckage onto the median. Like we've already started to say what we'll say over and over: We knew the whole time. Chair was too heavy. Rope too frayed. Too thin. Nah we knew. No shit we knew. You think we're stupid?

Benjamín Naka Hasebe Kingsley
The Hapa Anthem

> *I move with the elegance of an African elephant.*
> —Killer Mike, "Run The Jewels"

Badass top feeders. Real North Philly
boys.
    We were a tribe of concrete Natives
pigeon feathered   Latino Whiteys
Burnt Rice wannabees:

    block boy skid stains   &   *hijos of scarecrows*

they called us   brown

enough to smear an imagined girlfriend
    & her white panties. "The Christo
Rey Sharks"   we monikered ourselves.
As if we wanted to run
    far away but not yet forget our mothers—Christ,

    we wanted to be Papi Chulos, we wanted to kaboom
    (not bloom) into their language of how to make a home

        of dimpled hipbones. We supplicants eager
for tales of human humidors   filtered
through mocha cigars
    & the sheen of yellow teeth
    smoking on & on about the rudder of their tongues.

So we bowed
our mohawks our buzz cuts our sick fades

& we prayed
                    for jewels: encrusted fingers cresting
                              ten-ringed & gold our necks thick

          we bound our own feet
                              with colorful shoelaces
like the lashings of a newborn
          kite soaring high above the Schuylkill

                              we dangled from our bronzed Achilles

Our spindly limbs unwound with age, & again we prayed
          for stereo systems   loud
                              enough to outrun cop sirens
          hatcheting their red
                    whites & past our saggy blue
                              jeans   past our sandwiched crust
of uncut curb & we beat
          the tar across
          each other's faces & gleaming bone-shot
we came into
          our own heart's leaking.
                              Gaggles of fists we circled up
                              in that apartment complex basement
                              or this moon-gilded lot

empty.

& we spun each other's heads like well-oiled weathervanes.

We taught ourselves
          lessons we would be learning decade after

each decanting
                    finding ourselves

unable to lift and light
            the wet firewood of our arms

& find the actuation to pray again

for
fingers
reaching
just above the parapet.

Sarah Bates
Blue Rhino

This is the sound of caterpillars burning.

The passenger rear tire with a screw in its left side and the wolf in its own mouth. This is the last letter I wrote you. The first love coming back and the elephant leading me there.

The letter I never sent.

Bags hang from rotting trees, bodies fall to the feet of Virginia dogwood. The monarch spills across Appalachia and the smallest white rhino learns to walk along the coast.

This is me standing under the world's largest mounted specimen and you don't even know. The sign above me says the 24,000 lb. African Bush elephant was fifty-five years old when Josef J. Fenykovl came to hunt.

This is the distance between six white rhinos and the oldest love. My heart catching the train to the Smithsonian and a butterfly in my hair.

Bullets reach sky, the dolphin smells its own blood, every elephant comes home headfirst.

This is my friend telling me to pose for a picture, but all I see are swollen hands, his fingertips around the wrong neck, someone else's body at the top of the moat.

Every time I bump into a stranger, I see the deer's eyes between broken
limbs. Fiberglass made of painted ivory.

This is Harambe dying, Masamba wobbling, you talking to God at
25,000 feet. Me in the passenger seat above the Three Sisters just so I
could send you a picture.

Between tusks too heavy to mount, I follow the sound of heavy rains.
Beneath the mystery in water, the rocks unknown, I know the age
of honeybees. I see the seal puking up curdled milk and the swallow
thrown out of its own nest.

This is you telling me how the trees would fall asleep. How Teddy would
leave behind the bear and bring home someone else.

How the elephant would cross the river singing, but the children would
be too afraid to play.

This is my heart at the museum feeling too much.

One of the largest living mammals, the sign reads, *this rhinoceros is cur-
rently endangered.*

My heart in the shallow burrows where penguins lay their eggs.

Former President Roosevelt collected this specimen in 1909.

My heart writing poems about Nola on the train to the zoo.

"I speak of Africa and golden joys."

I was buying a ticket to San Diego Safari Park for the second time.

My dad used to burn caterpillars out of our front yard's trees. How he would wait for dusk to settle, and then light matches to them. I couldn't see their eyes, but I could imagine their moving bodies, pitch black and bright yellow, it was the smell of plants burning.

Sometimes I'd lie in bed and imagine them waking up to the flames.

Sometimes I'd bury them beside the same tree that burned.

This is my heart snow-covered in summer.

My heart at the foot of dogwoods making no sense.

Sitting at a blue table inside Little Italy, you pour my coffee into yours. I tell you how I can't stop writing about floating horns, her face on the other side. How now there are only three. You ask if I'd write about the second engine if you showed it to me.

I come home headfirst, I say, smelling the coffee black, running from the people on the train.

How you nudged me off the sidewalk because it's something your grandpa would do.

In 1909, Roosevelt made a deal with The Smithsonian. They would fund an expedition to east Africa and he would bring back big game for the museum's collection.

With a river craft, two sailboats, and some rowboats, he'd travel hundreds of miles down the Nile to Lado Enclave, hundreds of miles to one white rhino.

He planned to shoot two family groups, one for the Smithsonian and another that he had promised to a sculptor and taxidermist working at the American Museum of Natural History.

Roosevelt, who was known for being a conservationist, knew the white rhino was already nearing extinction, but felt the species was inevitably doomed, and it was important for him to collect specimens before it went extinct.

In the end, he shot five, another four killed by someone else. As game, rhinos were known for being unimpressive. Most were shot while waking up.

During the spree, sixty foot flames swept through red sky and elephant grass. Roosevelt and his men waking to the aftermath of apocalypse.

This is me in our hometown making sidewalk from the ash of ivory tusks.

Waiting for Skyfari, I read about fewer wolves. Caribou hunters leaving them behind to die. How sometimes they'd spill for a week and no one would know.

They eat coyotes alive, you tell me, how they'll take a bite out of the elk's back leg before it's had time to lift its second antlers. Before it's learned to cross the river. This is me 16,000 feet above Banff telling a stranger about the snare around its neck, the smell of rotting blood and the ivory ash covering our front yard's trees, and how sometimes the zoo is the only place I can go to be this sad.

You talk when you cease to be at peace with your thoughts

At the top of Marble Canyon, I see rainbows in dogwoods, orange mud across manmade grass. A couple asks why I do it alone. I say sometimes the forest has to die. The wolf killed in its sleep.

And in much of your talking, thinking is half murdered

I say sometimes the only way to African Plains is through spilling ochre.

The first time I read about Roosevelt, he was on a hunt for a bear. How she was 225 lbs. and mangy looking, but by the time he got to her, he just couldn't do it. He asked a friend instead, and chose a knife to put her out of her misery. He couldn't shoot something that had already been through such a fight.

This is you calling as soon as the train stopped, putting on your green suit and asking me what it means.

This is my heart at the table waiting to say blue. My heart missing the 5:30 bus and carrying Gibran.

I was just so sad, I tell you.

For even as love crowns you so shall he crucify you

I'm just so sad, I would say to the snow. I just want to be friends again. For months I fell asleep to all the animals awake. For months, you never said anything.

Even as he is for your growth so is he for your pruning

Months later at the Smithsonian, I pass a stuffed grizzly. Her arms lifted as if to fight.

This is me Googling "the saddest things happening in the world right now" eight months after you left.

"Jane Goodall Says Zoo Had No Choice but to Kill Harambe the Gorilla"

This is me moving to Michigan and you didn't even know.

He may have been protecting the boy and putting an arm around him.

Jane in Gorilla Forest waiting to push send.

But when people come into contact with wild animals...

Then five days later, the email in her outbox.

RE: "Complex Questions"

This is my heart buried thirteen feet in Elephant Valley.

This is my heart writing to tell you: "Countdown to extinction: Only six northern white rhinos left on Earth."

I see Harambe in his birthday hat. Nola passing out forks and Masamba licking Funfetti icing off the second engine. A couple sitting beside me asks how I do it alone.

This is me waking up to a flat tire and you falling asleep in our hometown.

This is me driving through grizzlies, through avalanche zones, through Asian Savanna and tusks worth more than platinum and gold.

Me in Gorilla Forest trying not to think about love.

Teddy and Jane sharing a grilled cheese sandwich above the trees.

How once I wrote to you about Polar Frontier, but I ran out of stamps.

This morning a shooter went into a nightclub in Orlando and killed forty-nine strangers. I'm telling my dad about Masamba when it comes on the news.

Months after I'd been writing about one white rhino, months after Oregon and Paris, months after I told you I just couldn't be friends anymore.

I can't stop writing about what I can't do.

Months after Nola died in San Diego.

How do we write about what isn't happening to us?

Months after you moved there to fly helicopters in the sun.

What hurts most—how it keeps coming back.

Months after I'd compare a rhino dying to the gun going off.

How I would write to sidewalks covered in snow.

My dad sips from his coffee mug, asks if there's still a can of ant spray under the kitchen sink.

This is me trying to write about Harambe, trying to make sense of Masamba being born and Harambe being shot, how forty-nine people are dead.

I don't know if you've heard about it yet, if you've put on your green suit, or if you're still sleeping.

But when I speak to you, there's the bridge to a picnic table. A sun drawn.

Sometimes I wake up to the monarch's wings between my teeth.

There's the way I was then, and the way I am now.

Sometimes I stare at my coffee until it becomes the second engine.

There's how many are praying and how many are crying.

Sometimes I drive three thousand miles to spill across African Plains.

How many are on their way to God.

This is my heart writing to everyone but you.

I'm afraid the trees are always awake. That the caterpillars will always burn. I'm afraid I'll never really know the age of honeybees. The color of butterflies spilling.

I'm afraid their bodies were identical, formless and still.

Michael Wasson
Self-Portrait as 1879–1934

It has darkened here only because the light inside
the room. Now place your hand there. See. That—

no, this—this is your face & so: *what are you*
but a citizen of this nation you were born into

by no hands of your own. Like the architecture
of briefly lit chapels, you stand here so silent

you're already another century broken
in two. Your mouth looks just like your father's

when he was still alive, crying. Four white walls
in the dark. How his skin felt of scratched chalk-

board with each new written version of him
now so American: his name sparing his one blood-

red life. & see your mother kneeling at this quiet
cage of crushed windows that held the last image

of her black hair. Say you see nothing in this
language & everything inside *'iníise pewíski, ne'é.*

ne'é? This tongue of animals you give to the open
night. Like a lungful of gnashed syllables rusted

to the throat. Say *c'éewc'ew* like a promise made
of bone—because after the body, what's left

is bone. The jaw opened wide enough to say *your
name* like a wildfire spreading through your home-

land every summer when you are left to stand
in its pine forest. & god. The forest. Save me,

my lost savior. Save the boy who sees the blood
inside him. The forest. How it means: shadows

learning to breathe again—the disgraced light
here. It means all these branches are clotheslines

where nothing hangs anymore. It means you
touching the mirror is enough to crack apart

every America you've known since. It means no-
body is here. It means the ash in the dirt blown

to air was the braided hair of your ghosts longing
to welcome you back. Which is to say: yes, every-

one is here.

Lily Zhou
Obsession #1: Film with Railroad Tracks

It's summer & we're on a train to the city.
      I open my mouth & a gun appears
in my mother's hand. I open my mouth
      & the field outside the window bodies
all of its inhabitants without apology.
      In a film about train accidents, I play
my mother's ghost & laugh every time
      someone loses a finger. My favorite color
is granite & I live in the underbelly
      of the field, where the grass is cool
& the coyotes never stay for long.
      But it's summer now & my mother
shrines a rabbit I love into holiness
      & pressed flowers. My mother opens
her mouth & a horse spills out, a nameless
      creature that begs for my blood. I have
my mother's eyes & sometimes, her language.
      I pull fruit from the ribs of the rabbit
& feed it to the dogs. In the film, the field
      never forgives me for stealing its face.
The body never lives past the first gunshot.

Fatimah Asghar
How We Left: Film Treatment

[Establishing Shot]
Here's the image my aunty gave me: the street a pool of spilled
light & all the neighborhood children at my grandfather's knee.
The kids, turbaned or taqiyahed or tilakaad or not. When Jammu
still smelled of jasmine.

[Elevator Pitch]
Yes, I've heard your story—the man who saved my family
before they were my family. The boy who sat, crowned
at the cusp of my grandfather's light, who walked to their home
each day, long cigarette sheltered between his lips, belt
wrapped around books, swinging their shadows to the sun.

[Primary Research]
Mamun remembers it like this: clutching a suitcase of toys
when the men came, machetes swinging the sun red. The year
when we found out who we were & who we were not.
All the Muslims boarded on the bus. The Sikh men, laughing
as the women walked by, *You wanted your fairytale & now you'll get it.*

[Rationale]
What's a nation to the sky? It takes a lot of work to remember
we are nothing. What has history given us but a bad home?
A legacy of men who've bloodied the soil. Some other land
to call country, some other snippet of sky to pretend we own.

[Secondary Research]
If my mom was still alive she'd tell it like this: clean, lean legs

pounding to ground. Blades catching the light. Her limbs lost
in the long grass. Her hand above, searching for someone's
to hold. The red rain falling on the leaves. The ground, a ruby
river she wished to swim in.

[Working Title]
Pakistan, a Disneyland for believers. The fairytale promised
land of prayer mats and ladoo. Fat chum chums dripping with pink
coconut syrup & all the rupees to buy them. Land of jobs & lamb
so tender it slides off the bone. Land of cannons at Ramadan's magrib
& nights bouncing with mehndi-ed feet. Borrowed Earth-heaven:
home in our own image.

[Legal & Ethical Considerations]
History didn't give me a blueprint for loving you, but here I am
70 years after you marched across a blood-soggy field, building
your altar. History didn't give you a blueprint for loving
us: but there you were, guiding through the tall grass, machete clearing
a red path, eyes towards the forest. Ready to swallow us whole.

[Character Breakdown]
They aren't soldiers, just men. Men with machetes who wear
matching shirts. Men who aren't soldiers, but walk like they are.
These aren't refugees, just families, vacationing to the Promised
Land. We aren't at war. Just neighbors who like to kill each other.

[Sample Dialogue]
You wanted your fairytale & now you'll get it—I know that man—
my teacher—our favorite—this bus goes right—right—left—did
you pack the attah—we'll come back when—yes—but Kashmir
is our—what's a home anyway—I know that man—the fairy
tale's a dust—a prick at the wheel—golden thread—bus gone left.

[Audio Element: Silence]
My auntie talks of the apple orchards. The fruit she piled into her arms
the backyard's jasmine petals perfuming the whole neighborhood.
& my grandfather, yes, she loves the story of my grandfather, teaching
the neighborhood children while all the streetlights fireflyed the night.

[Constraints]
Even with all this light, I can't see past the stories of my family.
The stories of a country I've never lived in, the sins of a land
mine & also not mine breaking my spine. All the streetlights
cast shadows as hot as blood. Careful not to wander too long
in the darkness. That's when we'll never come back.

[Contingency]
I'm a bad researcher: I don't know your name, what you said
other than taking my family off the bus once we arrived at the park
-ing lot full of death. This is a love letter, I think. You're a murderer
I think. Tell me what happened after. Did you save us, walk back
& slaughter the rest? What's your fairytale, then? *Pakistan Murdabad!*

[Target Audience]
Everyone wants Kashmir but no one wants Kashmiris. Kiss me
& taste survival. The metal pulp of my tongue. Aren't I a miracle?
A seed pulled from a family that survived the slaughter & the slaughters
to come. I think I believe in freedom, I just don't know where it is.
I think I believe in home, I just don't know where to look.

[Narrative Device: Flash Forward]
In America they slaughtered a Sikh temple because they thought
them us. Here we all become towelheads, amorphous fears praying
to a brown god. They don't know our history, its locked doors
& heavy whispers. Americans are confused, perpetually.
It could almost be funny, if they didn't own guns.

[Narrative Device: Flashback]
Let us bring back the books, belted in your hand, swinging
their shadowed loved across your body. Let us remember you
as a schoolboy: handsome, sucking a cigarette, never worrying
about your lungs or your gut—old man fears hanging on some
distant clothesline. Let us hold a moment of this, forever.

[Visual Element: Filtered Light]
Mamun remembers it like this: the bus turning left. Right. Left?
The lot of parked busses, mountains of Muslim bodies hacked to death.
The flies, finding their dinner. Kissing cold skin. A brown shirt
& red crusted machete, running towards them. My grandfather's eyes
wide. The boy who used to sit by his knee, now a man.

[Visual Element: Camera Swing]
You're the god of small slaughters. The man who would not let
his teacher die. We won't even get a paragraph in the history books.
I'll write to you forever. Does your family know? What story
were they told? Are your grandchildren in Jammu still, throwing
rocks at the armies who stain the land?

[Property Rights]
Everyone wants Kashmir, a crown on a useless throne, a ruby
fed by blood, carved from machete. The past is a land I do not know
I can't read the street signs when I wander here. I make up what
I can't see. I want a land that doesn't want me. I love a land that doesn't
exist. I love a man who saved my family by taking our home.

[Denouement]
Here's the image my uncle gave me: the long march through the forest
after, his mother's plea to Allah piercing the trees like a strangled bird.
My mother's eyes blank, as he held her hand, his siblings' squeals drying
in their throats. & there, in the horizon: a new country, a broken
promise, brimming with the same death.

[End Credits]
In another life, could we still be neighbors? Could you have been
my uncle, throwing me over your shoulders when I was a baby?
Your wife, hand-sewing me a velvet frock for my birthday. & when
I grew up, I could have taught your children's children's children until
the streetlights came on, until our neighborhood crowded with night.

Alfredo Aguilar
On This Side of the Desert

raul & i drive by a yellow sign   that reads *cuidado—no exponga
su vida a los elementos—no vale   la pena.* we pass   a mountain where,
tucked away in a place   that the relentless sun cannot   reach, the
direction & miles   left to the border   are scratched into a
boulder.   raul tells me that yesterday, under a creosote,   he
found a knapsack holding   only a light bulb & a battered bible.   the
body was nearby,   so far from god. the legs   consumed by cramps.
the skin wrung   of its sweat. all the water escaping   the
body to try & keep   it cool. the clothes stitched   onto his skin by
the sun. last night's   full moon a final eucharist his mouth   could
not reach. he had a name, santos. he also had a wife. or maybe   it
was a mother, or a sister,   or a daughter. the wallet didn't say.
we stop at a white crucifix   staked into the ground   where
there are no roads & leave twelve bottles   of water & twelve pears.
raul tells me   that he once found   an entire skeleton in torn
clothes,   the sneakers still tied   to its feet. on our way back to
the orto lado   a flash flood rushes across   the road in front us.
we stop,   step out, & face it. we leave   the truck running, the
speakers aching   *y volver volver.* sweat collects at the base   of the
gold crucifix necklace   underneath my shirt.   *the rains are short
but so heavy,*   i say. *right raul?*   nests of gila woodpeckers
poke   their heads out of a saguaro. i look   at their curious
eyes.   *raul,* i say & the saguaro   blooms. i stare back   at the
flood. i say my mother's name,   *cristina,* & desert marigolds crack
through a boulder. i say   my father's name, *martin,*   & all the
novena candles   in the bed of the truck   are aglow.   i say *santos*
& in a pair of footprints   in the sand a man is built up   from the
part of his body   that touched this earth most. i say the names   of

my tias, tios, primos, & a bronzed mass   dressed in white rises from
the rushing flood.   their backs are turned to me,   they wear my
family's shoulders. they head north. before them   the white obelisk
marking   the line in the ground   crumbles. before them
the metal   fences dissolve like mist.

Andres Rojas

From the Lost Letters to Matias Perez, Aeronaut

I imagine what you saw—a boulevard
of moonlight on water, waves

like names on a chart,
your absence, like weather, a given.

My father disappeared
into another country

when I was five—why
not you, a hundred years before?

My first memory is him.
He carries me against his neck,

the beach receding as he walks us
into a life I don't yet see.

Sometimes I wish
that were the last of him

I kept. Of what's beyond us,
we know nothing, or we know

enough, the particulars of loss:
sand, the westering sun,

a wind-seized balloon,
the sea.

—Nominated by *AGNI*

Erin L. McCoy

Futures

We drank champagne on the eve of   The moon stuck out its jaw, slowly   swallow is the
color of victory   we upped rents in Monopoly   you grew a garden, especially tulips
the Cascades are hazel at dusk only   the moon opened its jaw, slowly   In your neck, a
nodule   like a tulip's bulb   mostly   cloaked and strange to its body   champagne
is the color of sputtering earth   the bulb with its pale hairs   moon-tentacles the color of
:   you have a knot in your throat and what's shrinking   is not the knot but   the moon
bared all its teeth, slowly   the gravel in the bulb-bed not   mule teeth gleaming with
calcite, too   dirt-common to polish clean like   the mole's snout   is common like
the skin on its eyes   is too like   lymphocytes in their milk-white teaspoons   Once
we found sour   nickels in the grass, pressed them into our   cheeks   to see what
grew Today the doctor said a sour   spoon has tunneled out   a house   in you
The moon is swallowing, like a python, the mouse-brown cloud, slowly   And we line up
champagne corks   little top hats   Life   is civilized, don't forget that   now that
you have a garden, especially   tulips   Now I own all the railroads and every
passenger pays me handsomely but you   wink and glim past me,   you build hotels
and clutch every property   to your sternum, even   the poorest   The loam in your
garden is porous and mole-holed and moles   survive it, although ice   has come very
early   It's said they can't see but even with skin   spannering their vision

they glimpse the patter   of light, know the seasons churn   the slant of moonlight like

a glass cutter   The Cascades are bruise-blue at dusk only   that is, too   early

Our moon shuts its mouth slowly   lumps of once-cloud tunneling   down its body

fisheyeing the stars that crawl over its skin

Bernard Ferguson

on eagerness

after Aziza Barnes

consider the centipede   and its slow progression of legs   across the
cold kitchen tile   then consider my sister   the sharpest blade   out
the drawer   and in her hands   how she will not rest   until she
splits   the bronze of the creature in two   until she stands over its
carcass   to watch the last twitch   of its last moving leg   both
of them   anxious for safety   the whole game   has always been
of wit   and will   some day, i am to face   the beast   and its line of
weapons   stretched long   and deep   into the night   i know
no other way   to prepare   than to sweat myself golden   with
every second   of breath that i am gifted   i know it's
best   to swallow the meal whole   before it sprouts a belly   and
grows desperate   to fill it   i know it's best   to leap for what's
mine   even if there is a sidewalk   and its concrete   made to split my
lips   promise me a passport   that would grant me a   life   in
this country of   loving faces   and i will hand over   whatever
dignity   still lines my skin   as a sacrifice   promise me a
lover   that won't turn to ash   in the face of the sun   and i
will turn my back on the world   as i know it.   a woman
once   dragged all of her desire   across three state lines   to show its
tender back   to the face of my roommate   and when i asked   if
she would be doing it again   he said he just wished   she
wasn't   so *eager*   wished she had been ravenous   without
baring   her teeth   don't we all want the monster   to control its
hunger   until we have learned   how to lick its horns   and
savor?   there is something   about witnessing   the sum
of all our wanting   for the first time   how it draws the tongue
out   and onto the chin   i do not wish   to play coy   with my
lips   and how they can swallow   an entire body   without killing
it   i have been contained   to the edges of this skin   for decades
too long   another second   is asking   so much of me

Mary Angelino
Unanswered Questions about the War

Where is the sky-
blue scarf Nonno first saw you in

at fourteen—fifteen?—and he fell in love?
What happened after

you ate all the chickens?
Where did your mother hide you

when the soldiers came? What did they want
besides food? And your sister,

who years later would put her own daughter's eye out
with a broom—*la incidente*, I know—

where did she hide? How many
people died—I mean, how many people

did you know who died? What happened
to the village priest, his rings shining

in dad's black and white communion photo?
What did the soldiers take besides food?

What didn't you have to sell? Will you show me
what you kept, what they let you keep?

Yuki Tanaka
Death in Parentheses

He came home with his right leg made a bit shorter
but they didn't notice. A landmine did it, he said
to himself, and I was the only one who heard him
because I followed him everywhere like a son.
He hobbled when no one was looking,
and I hobbled behind him.
When he plucked an iris, I plucked the one next to it,
and we thought of purple evening clouds.
When he killed a butterfly, he'd take off the wings first,
then crush it with his fingers and smell it.
I tried to catch one, but it flitted away.
He wanted to build a huge power plant
to keep us from disappearing. I nodded
and pointed out all the recent deaths, how quick they were,
tomatoes not as plump as they used to be,
the maple trees discolored, their branches
like veins with no fat around them.
All this, he decided, meant we needed new things.
But I disagreed on this: why new, why not
old me, I who have lived here for many years
even before he was born, but he didn't listen.
Mosquitoes come and go,
full and happy. Outside the window, the plant
looms over the village. It looks prettier than I thought,
which makes me want to kiss it, but I know it will
burn my lips and I won't be able to speak to anyone
with my charred mouth. I saw him
dressed up for a meeting, and they shouted,

blaming him for his empty head,
for wanting too much. The next time I saw him
he was in bed, old and delirious.
He opened his eyes, and held my hand
for the first time, and said, Don't push yourself, come back
alive. He was buried in his ever-vanishing land,
and I flew off into my friendless life.

—Nominated by the Michener Center for Writers

Zaina Alsous

Leave

A hijacked plane in 1969 lands in Damascus. This means a plane was unable to fly
away, to Tel Aviv. I read about the incident in the autobiography of Leila Khaled.
This book is out of print. This means it is difficult to find her first hand account in text
though much is written about her. I wanted to write a poem about Leila: a hero,
or terrorist, depending on who you ask. Dareen is the name of a woman,
who lives under house arrest. This means she is unable to leave her home.
Israeli officials categorize her as a threat, she calls herself a poet.
The speaker is an important part of a poem. A rule of poetry, try
not to let the reader out of a poem. At this point I will disobey and say
you are free to go if you choose. Choice is a complicated part of describing
Palestinian heroes or terrorists. The Israeli and Palestinian *conflict* is studied
in class. The word *conflict* in English, defined as "a serious disagreement."
If you are still here, doesn't that sound fair? Two sides, equally at fault,
each making a choice. Three generations later, I still do not know
how to explain choices. A place was left behind. A place I have never seen.
This means I still do not know how to write myself
into existence. Three boys form a tributary of blood, on a beach in Gaza, elsewhere
a contained border, a family of bones, without broth; these will be described as incidents.
The difference between violence and incidents in a *conflict,*
depends on the speaker. What word would you choose to begin?
Nakba translates as "Catastrophe." Ha'atzmaut, "Independence."
Though Hebrew and Arabic share yawm or yohm,
for *day*. Alan Dershowitz and other Israeli historians argue
it was a choice of Palestinians to leave the land in 1948.
Argue, a word used when choosing an explanation about why things are.
History is a collection of choices. I have also inherited memories.
Pink prayer beads on the counter. Creases in white fabric, black threads
embroidering live skin. Memories do not always obey

the lines of history's choices. My grandfather fled the land
when he was eight years old, leaving his mother at home.
This means he never saw her again. Many will continue to argue
leaving and never returning is a choice, not a violence.
A poem, depending on the speaker, an act of incitement
to violence. Concrete left in the throats of children, a mother's final glance,
a segregated beach, a segregated sun; it is all just
a great misunderstanding, a *conflict*. I have changed my mind.
I am leaving
you and this poem behind. A choice, I choose, this time.

Xandria Phillips
Social Death, an Address

with a nod to Terrance Hayes

I write to you from the predicament of Blackness.
You see, I've been here all my life and found
on the atomic level, it's impossible to walk through
most doorways. I can, however, move through
walls. I write to you from the empty seat that isn't
empty, from a tenure-track train to Angola
Penitentiary. I write to you when a feel is copped.
I write myself out of bed. I write to you as the spook
who sat by the door. I write to you from Olivia Pope's
apolitical mouth. One of us gets liminal every
so often, slides through a doorway like a slice of rye
or pumpernickel into the toaster. Toast is a grain
cremated twice. Once through its skin. Once cross
sectioned. I am here because I could never get the hang
of body death, though its been presented to me,
like one would offer a roofied cocktail or high-interest
loan. I am only here because I started eating again.
I am only here because I am ineligible to exist
otherwise. I'm only here. When your mother went
appliance shopping she had the option of purchasing
my hands. When your boyfriend went out for groceries
he returned with my breasts in a twist-tied bag.
When my name is read aloud, the vowels become
spaces for a man to enter. I'm only here because
I left and returned through an Atlantic wormhole.
In the American version, Eurydice is knocked up
before the viper injects her with death. In the
American version, the fetus is Black. Eurydice dies.

Her death is not physical. In the American version,
the fetus dies, and its death is physical. In the American
version, Orpheus's lyre is a gun. Eurydice thinks
of doctors, or, rather a cold hand. It feels like one
is sliding its sterile nails over the curtains of her womb.
Once, a healer's hands passed through my flesh,
and I went on trial for stealing ten fingers. My spoon
scrapes the bottom of a bowl, and it sounds
like a choir of my siblings naming stars after
their favorite meals. Physicists are classifying new
matters and energies. Dark matter, Black flesh are in
high demand, and we never see a penny. I urge you.
If you see a sister walk through walls or survive
the un-survivable, sip your drink and learn to forget
or love the taxed apparition before you.

—Nominated by *Nashville Review*

Keith S. Wilson
God Particle

You were the smallest thing. Think
of the terrified play

of rabbits in the grass before the street:
fractional, they are

ants reverse-engineering the desperate flapping
of the land. Even less.

They are mindless
atoms unaware of themselves or the heart

between matter and time. You were smaller and more
precious than that. If you imagine

them littler than eyelashes—their tissue paper carapace,
thorax—all of it—the bones of ships

under glass—if you can imagine the elements of those atoms, of those ants
and rabbits, as not the skin of the observable universe,

but the whisper upon which we built a hearth,
you'll understand. Call it want,

or dependence or sleep. Call it eventide or
home; how to summarize a galaxy

with a night
—we are impossible

to fix. Dust motes and a million paths of light.
I know.

Eventually it all comes down to an
admission.

Whatever my failings—didn't I come to it,

              eventually?

Meghan Maguire Dahn
Never Do Housework with Imperfect Intent

When I was a housewife
I was the finest egret.
I would wait all day

for any train—yours
or any of a hundred commuter's
as they flit their course on Narragansett.

I'd wade the anticonvulsant radius,
free of rope and sympathy.
We made a runt. Our glass half

empty. On the heirloom Blue Willow
I painted a beast. Each on each.
The withering work. My form

had been perfect. Now I cover
the mirrors. To approach god
build a charge with every coiling,

every uncoiling atom. *Left left left.*
Heart heart heart. I will chew
this secret when it grows full.

I will fold small clothes with my beak.

K. T. Landon
What We See, What Sees Us

The truck fishtails down the mountain road,
snow flying past the headlights like galaxies.

We hit the brakes just feet before the two deer,
who pause and stare at us, blinking

in the wet, unnatural light, their bodies blurred
in ragged winter fur. They turn away slowly,

set their faces against the roar of the snow,
going on because they must, attuned

to something else—not memory or hope—some
understanding with the frozen stars, some wholeness

that persists behind the skin of the world.

M.K. Foster
Memoria Animalia

—or how when you open up to clear and gut the just-killed
animal, the heart is usually still beating. First, clean-sever

the head-trophy; then take whatever else you want and leave:
fair game—something meant to share spoils with the land,

but often, more like not-wanting the extra weight; body after
wasted body found frosted while walking after hunting season,

wet spine and rib patches barely beginning to breach, glitter
what's left of the skin: bone-lights like damp porch lamps

through black field grass, the cardinal torches for which you once
longed when lost as a child, ivory flares to which you still run,

bolt from the long-dark yard behind your eyes skinned
wide open, deep in those nights like the bones that break

the teeth off the saw: sleepless, stateless, fucking for warmth,
waiting on the fatted world with the empty patience of axes.

Caitlin Roach
American Landscapes

[*after the women of the maquiladoras*]

in the city opposite the city of factories
my nephew readies for preschool.

his skin is clean, marked only by a scrape
on his knee from when he fell chasing a boy

chasing a ball around the school lot. at night
after his bath, his father chases him around the house.

in the morning his mother drops him off
at the school on the hill next to the church

overlooking the ocean. he finds his place in line
of other children, twenty twinned and quiet claps

of twitching, pale-winged fleas marching in order
up the asphalt hill, slapping in chorus. behind him, a girl

watches her shadow all the way up until her
mark in line rounds the building at the top

that steals it right back. as if it were a gift
to begin with. in school they are taught obedience,

manners, about god, how to pray. yesterday
my nephew appeared with ash smeared on his forehead

from the priest who bent to convey his inaugural
recognition of sin with such gladness my nephew

thought he'd done something
right to receive it.

⁓

each time a woman enters
the maquiladora her nose bleeds.

I push the material into the round machine. with one hand I push,
with the other I remove. I push, remove, push, remove, push—

⁓

all these mouths have already named all those
who said nothing, who see now still the lead-laden rio,

the sores on arms and legs of their children
when babies were born without fingernails

yet scratch and scratch all day and night long
and still they say nothing, retreating in instinct

from the ghost hollowing of itself in the bodies
of all these others. for twenty years

wind has howled through the rusty hulls' rotted-out
hearts. they call it the cry of the barrels *can you hear it*

confronting each day who haven't the luxury
to look away from what we can no longer.

some say structural vulnerability has no room
in a poem like this but what kind of luxury is that.

there are holes in everything
from where the lead's burned through.

⁓

bodies ford the river doubled in rush
when they release the waste with the rains

for disguise but everyone knows what time it is. still,
there is nowhere else to cross to walk to the big white box

where blood will fall from their bodies and
are you enjoying your television?

⁓

my nephew jumps in puddles for feeling
the force of his body displacing

everything that's under it. *do you understand
the implications of pushing everything out*

from where it belongs I ask him. he just looks up,
grabs my hand and tells me to jump with him so I do.

⁓

six thousand tons of lead slag left
laying exposed, taken up in the light

that rushes the women to where they returned
each day and night, wondering of their children

did my son get home okay? how is he? has he eaten?
entombed now in a concrete slab where balls slam

by a sea of sored hands. one goes bouncing
and five bodies chase it. to be sure

they know nothing of mast years, know only
the ambient sound of wire lines zapping

in sewage where a stray ball lodges and is retrieved
by a child innumerous, in the slush where a four-year-old

girl's body broke. *it entered here in her leg
and came out through her cheeks* her father said.

~

white puffs blow from a tower and flit through the air. *some kind of ash
is falling* a woman says as she runs with her shirt

pulled over her face. *I feel like a Christmas tree, all covered in snow.*
on the other side of the iron spine I twirl with my nephew in a plaza

of a mall under soapy clumps blown out of a machine's mouth.
this is all he knows of snow. it is Christmastime in San Diego.

~

*when we talk of globalization, we see that these companies can go anywhere
in the world. when the government shut the factory, the owner fled. he went*

to San Diego. he owns the parent company there and reports a million dollars
of profit each year. who is more to blame: the government corrupted

by the multinationals or the multinationals
that pay our government to break the law?

            ~

within globalization, a woman factory
worker is like a commodity. if that commodity

is not productive, if she's not attractive for globalization
because she starts to defend her rights, then they look for that

commodity elsewhere. they depart with their hands full
and leave us with ours empty.

            ~

they'd hire them if they could women on the other side
say to each other but *only the words remain, floating in the air*

like ash and the EPA like a broken record
resolves to *no significant impact.**

---

   *   The italicized portions on this page and the prior three pages are transcripts of dialogue from the 2006 documentary *Maquilapolis*.

[on an American Airlines flight to Las Vegas, Nevada]

the woman I loved is no longer.
she escaped her body and went else-

where, her moult still wet
like the road these wheels slow to

I've been combing for something
to put in its place. I was the one

who stayed tomorrow to hold the flames
so you could see by the bluing heat

that could never give us
the definition of white, don't you

remember. in the room you woke
I knelt to gather the scattered flashes

of glass a mirror dispelled
when I heard the news. on a clear night

the prong-horned antelope can see
the rings of Saturn we learned

when we crossed state lines and
haven't been the same since. imagine

killing something that can see
into the universe I whispered. on a plane

I sat next a hunter who showed me
his kills unprompted. glutting,

the great-horned owl freezes his own
and thaws them when ready to feed

he told me. when I spoke of the antelope,
he quieted for a moment then swiped

to a picture of his comely twenty-
something-year-old daughter posed

in a neon bikini. *isn't she something*
he said, and looked hungry.

[*on the 11, Albuquerque, New Mexico*]

this morning on my bus route to work
a man holding a gallon bag

full of heroin asked me directions
to San Mateo. I told him I was going there

too but the truth is I stopped praying
a long time ago. he was begotten

of a man so obsessed with form
it broke him and so now lives

in collapse. I knew an immigrant
activist who did a four-month stint

building a prison in Texas
when he was sixteen. he'd just crossed

and knew not yet of brinks but needed
something to do with his body.

he went to the edge of a cave
to hear the millioned wingbeats of bats

outpouring, just to hear the sound, just to see
something erupt from a dark center.

[under wisteria on Marquette Ave]

despite what everyone says
about a goddamn dream

there's mourning at all these
nodes of asylum. somewhere

a lapwing *claps itself to the bole
of a tree,*[†] echoing its name

to sweeten what wants
what's in its scrape

in the ground but never comes. down
the block, a hysterical heap of purple

lets loose like a slouched mouth
slurring its fragrant mess as a man

sits under it, narrowly alive, drawing
the last bit out from the spoon's small pool

while sweet williams break through
the alyssum around him, and despite this

country's best effort,
still exists.

---

†   paraphrased from J.A. Baker, in his book *The Peregrine*.

[Friendship Park, USA]

so

much

arrives in

form of see-

ing something

other than what's

there, like a shadow

arriving first, but when

I saw foam sacs perched on

spines of sick weed that summer

I saw them. there was no way to mis-

take the spit for something other than co-

cooned. I breathed, they trembled but stayed

put. what hid lived in just enough fear to remain.

on this side of the border, the body at the most-west-

ern edge of the wall splitting even the ocean looked latched

but knew better than to make contact, to stay out of the bishop's

straight shot. signs nobody could read said nothing the threat of just

living didn't warn already. between the three walls a pair of bodies moved

measured, aware of their being watched by at least a body behind. who was watch-

ing the watcher watch me watch the man in front of me, peering through the crosshatch

iron mesh, a wall within walls, waiting for bodies beloved he knows he cannot touch to arrive on the other side. I moved toward the body I loved and touched it. how fucked. a small white cross

on the fence between fences marked a death before us or else all of the ones to still come here.

this space used to give more and before that could barely be counted as marked. years later

in White Sands, I'll see a darkling beetle I'm never meant to see sunned frozen on the

dunes. fish out of water. seeker of dark places, dweller in dark, some shock of a

missile must have exploded its tiny heart as it crossed the desert in the night,

its three-parted body stilling part by part. inch by inch this iron

hull corrodes of itself. up close, licheny sprawls bleed out from the

heart I know it does not have. to its north women are shackled

to hospital beds during labor, giving birth to their babies in

the presence of prison guards for passing through this

thing that protects as much as the man who denies

even the bluest blue absorbs everything around

it but itself.   acute failure.   I've spent years

studying blue.   we believe in three words

he said: *peace.   through.   strength.* but

even the land   will   depose it, its

makeup a sentence,   a mouth

summoning its own demise

by simply being *exposed*

to the air   that enters

this body §, and that

one, and that one

and that one.

---

§   paraphrased from a presentation given by essayist José Orduña,
author of *The Weight of Shadows: A Memoir of Immigration and Displacement.*

Samantha Deal
Litany According to the Laws of Heat in Southern Appalachia

In these parts the world arrives as if from underwater, less in focus
than it oughta be. Got our name from a blue you can't ever see

up close. Old folks say it's something in the trees that does it.
They sit out back all summer and chew silence. "Land Of The Blue

Smoke," "Aways Back Of The Beyond": we got a shit-ton of names
for what's far-off. August is a particular backwoods near-dark, hidden

is how we like it. Language of *might could* and *got gone,* speak as if unfolding
as if wandering off into the Pentecostal blue yonder. Think refraction, what happens

when sunlight has left one thing and moved into another. Think blood thick
as static, kin reverb—a dirt gone so deep it becomes a part of you

because nothing changes once you accept your fingernails
as they are, the earth beneath, dirt-stuck, uneven. Today is the sort of day

that makes whatever won't wash out seem as sacred as the high lonesome
claw hammer sound when someone says "homesick." Get down

on your denim knees and kneel to the ghost of asphalt & afternoon,
all those long shadows & backyard sprinklers, back-and-forth

of screen door & porch swing—childhood & all the haunting
that goes with it. You would like to remember those nights as barefoot-safe

and cricket-stark, but understand this: it was never a pool of water or oil out there
in the distance—only a displaced wave of light colliding with an exhaust pipe

or a neighbor's charcoal grill, only a reflection of sky. This is the gift of drought,
what people call Highway Mirage or Heat Haze, something slag-pile deep a-hum

beneath every acre of scorched land. Only a matter of what we need to see in order
for our world to make sense. We are sweat & salt, all of us—the same percentage

of magnesium in our blood as in the Atlantic. Take this place as you would
a sunburn: think naked, think skin, think sex—the kind you regret, but don't. Mirage

after mirage—the closest you will ever get to the apathy of ocean. As if the wild
blue yonder were anything but open, as if it were the sky that came down slurry-thick

& crystallized coal ash, all slow-like. Take this dirt as you would a breath of water.
Take it as you did that boy, when you were fifteen. How smooth the darksome feel

of him on your arms and legs—amazing, what we can do alone. To be part of something
that works until it doesn't. So go on and push at your optic nerve the way you would

with any Springhouse door that's heavy and hard to shut: our hands make sense of things
as best they can, but it's our eyes that must endure whatever blue savior rises up

from beneath this gravel pit. After all, who wouldn't want to remember wearing nothing
but that place, the streets and stores abandoned, an entire town gone out of business.

Kristina Martino
Kristina's World: After Wyeth

I feel every grass scratch in the field.
I yield to them. They yield to me. I feel
      the aftermath of dirt making indelicate
            my limp dress. I'm making a mess of my-

self, yes, but to crawl like this is to digress
the limbs in a cower outstretched
      like a tigress stalking—or, at least, palm
            after palm, part infant, part pet. I have

yet to consider the aerial view, the rarest
human vantage point, on plane with the hawk—
      I'm a vulnerable pack of flesh waiting
            for the beak-to-talon pickup. In my path,

a plethora of stalks have snapped
and stippled. No apologies for that. And no
      apologies for this. My lines leave a trail
            behind, the brittle elastics of straw half-

bounce back and slacken. Such is the embroidery
of a dragged body, living or dead. Like grazing.
      I alter the landscape. I pass brazen like a dead-
            weight rain storm cloud by fuscous rodents

and metallic insects. I wreak havoc on
intermittent anthills; I flatten an enterprise
      in seconds. There is no architect here. Barns
            are raised to be barns. And in them, I put my

livestock in. They live there, altar to the land.
Illuminating, fattening. At stake for me is meat
        and milk. Something as murky as the word *miracle*.
                At stake for them is grass and grains, the lingering

of the killing knife. I'm not tired. The trajectory
is interjectional, sliced. Like a bleach of gold-leaf
        in the black of sleep. Such is the scenic route.
                It's the same as the short-cut. The sun makes

my underlids lacteous as titanium white
when I shut my. When I undercut my eyes. I'm in
        a place like the place where the eyes go
                when they're closed. It's hollow. It's like to live

in a squint. A bird bone. Let it sink
in, a louse to the mind. Pounced upon. The crawl-
        space is endless, this here to which I'm inhered.
                Every blink is a bold move—to return to the ex-

panse of field as if it's filled with my eye-lashes
and a shield of drowning light. Farther afield are
        the thoughts I feel rather than think. I yield to
                them. They yield to me. In pink, I reach the house.

Eloisa Amezcua
Watching Underworld, Inc. *Episode 3: "Human Cargo"*

The Pima County Morgue,
approximately 110 miles

from my childhood home,
houses John Doe, Jane Doe,

[sexless] Doe. Dated remains
found in the Sonoran Desert—

nameless and alone. The medical
examiner holds a fragmented

cranium, points to where
the eyes would go.

/

I cross the border   on foot.
My father   waits for me

in the McDonald's   parking lot
one block   into America.

I stand   in the line
labeled   *Ciudadanos.*

/

Francisco, a people smuggler
in Nogales, says his secret

is training others
to hide and survive.

/

I don't remember much   from middle school
US history—   who lead the troops

that took   Fort Ticonderoga   or who forced
General Pemberton   to surrender in 1863—

but I remember   like yesterday
the sound of my mother's voice

practicing   the Pledge of Allegiance
before her   naturalization ceremony.

/

A Border Patrol agent
explains how after five days

on foot in the desert,
skin begins to split

from the burning sun—
flesh exposed and open.

Nothing can be done once
the breaking has started.

/

Gratitude is a word that comes to mind.

/

In Phoenix, Magdalena buys and sells
moneyless migrants wholesale—

their families unable to pay off cartel
trafficking rates. Three women/girls sit

one room over, faces hidden with pillow cases—
they're background. And Magdalena, she talks

a tough talk, says business is business
and business is good. Her face concealed

by a black bandana and mirrored sunglasses
reflecting the camera back into itself.

/

When the show's over,   I'll call my mother
just to hear   the sound of her voice.

Como estas?   she'll ask.   And I'll lie,
tell her things are fine   the way

she'd say   the same to her mother
thirty years before   when she moved

to this country   alone
with her husband.   I'm haunted

by that for her.   I moved thousands of miles
away   alone   just to feel

closer. Before   we hang up, she'll say
Dios te bendiga,   picture me signing myself

or kissing a crucifix   I can't bring myself
to wear.   A blessing I don't need

but I take it   anyways.

Leila Chatti
Motherland

What kind of world will we leave
                for our mothers? My mother

calls me, weeping. I am
                far and the country she gave

me could kill me. Or
                that's what she's saying, her voice

clumsy with tears—my mother
                who never cries, and so

for this, too, apologizes. Sometimes, more
                often, I want to mother

my mother. I've begun to
                wonder what it is like for her

to have four hearts
                outside her body, buried

in brown and fragile skin. *I never wanted this*
                for my children, my mother sobs

from a Michigan town
                where once men crowded in white

cloaks, their sons still
                there lingering at drug stores and gas pumps

with steely guns and colder eyes.
                What do you tell a mother

you love too much
                to lie to? My mother

named me Leila because it was a song
                white men played on air guitars, which meant,

she'd hoped, they couldn't hate me. *I'm so scared now*
                for Rachid, even with his blonde hair—

My mother thought her blood
                might protect us in this country

from this country, her fair genes and cast-
                aside Catholic god. Thinks now

she failed us as children because she only ever told us
                stories of monsters

we wouldn't recognize. Mother,
                I know these men

could be your brothers
                and do not blame you. She weeps.

I am far and the country
                monstrous. What kind of world

do we mother, knowing
        what it is, what it's capable of?

The long night stretches
        between her window and mine.

As if comforting a child, I say the word
        kind—as in, *the world is still*

kinder than we think. I think
        I believe it. *Mom* I say

stop crying—no one's leaving this world
        to anyone yet.

Bryce Berkowitz
Thank You, Forgiveness

I'll walk off remembering this:
I spent October alone, in that library
too proud to seek help; an old problem.
I slept on a couch and you sadly sung
until the evening crept in. But first, winter;
we crossed a frozen highway, hand in hand.
A meditation at sunrise: *soft is my heart.*
It's always over before I'm willing to admit.
So many I've lost count. But to marry oneself—that's new.
And tonight I gave a house key back.
Redbud petals bled from a branch. A nighthawk
on the windowsill. The piecemeal quality of memory.
What beauty left inside; how quietly hope blooms.

—Nominated by the West Virginia University
MFA in Creative Writing Program

Amanda Turner
What Clowns

My four-year-old daughter likes to tell me
how the world works.

*Make what you don't want
to make,* she says as she cuts
purple and yellow pieces of construction paper
into swords and bowls, and toppling vessels.
        That's creative.

*If you're off the fence,
you do bad work,* she continues
as she pastes these pieces together
into what she calls "The Big Mess."

I give her a plate of carrots and apples,
peanut butter on bread, milk.

Squirrels outside
collect their nuts, jump from one branch
to the next. Lou Reed sings,
*There's a bit of magic in everything
and then some loss to even things out.*

A year ago I told myself to stop doing
anything that takes everything
and doesn't mean everything.

So much food falls to the floor.

This. This is my favorite part.
Gene Kelly kicks his arms and legs out to the side
and lifts his smiling face up
to the driving rain.

What clowns but the graceful ones? a friend asks.

My daughter licks her peanut butter into hills and valleys.
She stares out the window.
Brightly colored firecracker boxes from Diwali
disintegrate into a soft pulp in the rain.

Death, she tells me,
*means half the body is flying
and the other half, apple seeds.*

She sips her milk.
Extends her hands for a napkin.
When I say, *Maybe God is energy,*
she says, *No boots.*

Shane Lake
No Crying in Baseball

When Billy dropped the pop-up,
       the record scratched, the earth stopped
spinning, galaxies froze. Little league was over,
       but Billy's dad had cancer so bad
he couldn't watch two pitches in a row
       without coughing, so we swallowed our anger,
each of us a star on the verge of explosion,
       our fires delayed. He didn't seem sick
in the parking lot after the game,
       saying "Goddammit, Billy, would you stop
crying? You're embarrassing yourself
       again." Billy didn't come to the team pizza party,
and later that summer we heard
       he and Jack Howard touched each other
just to see what it felt like.
       Billy said it wasn't weird
because they both had their pants on,
       that it was no different
than slapping someone's ass after a home run,
       but that's not what Tommy's older brother said,
so we stopped inviting Billy to sleepovers.
       Sometimes after everyone fell asleep,
I'd think about him and stare at the stars
       aglow in my room, a gift
he helped me stick to the ceiling.
       I'd wonder if being touched by someone else
felt the same as touching yourself,
       if it felt like looking at the magazines

Tommy's brother stole from 7-Eleven
   was supposed to feel, or if
it was something I hadn't learned
   the words for yet. My favorite song
that summer was "Cupid" by 112,
   but I hid the CD underneath my mattress,
listened through headphones, and always
   changed the channel if the video came on
and my friends were over,
   not the first time I had to kill
a part of myself to survive.
   Still had the scars from the way they laughed
when I said TLC was my favorite group.
   Now I was smarter.
I would never be Billy, whose family moved
   closer to the city hospital
so he never came back to school in the fall,
   wasn't there when we learned
Earth is the only planet with one moon,
   their rotations synchronous
like slow-dancing lovers. He was light-years away,
   and I never got to ask him
what it really felt like or say
   it's ok Billy I never really liked
playing baseball much anyway.

Jonah Mixon Webster

Excursus: A Reverie

Light tricks itself from the rim of my sleep // a drink hangs my head through the gap of a thin bottle // as if for no ordinary reason, two black birds collapse into the florid hem of this horizon // now the sudden weight of it // the thresh of my belly, blunt puckered in the sun // with no hum nor cloud do I come to you // O' object of your too-soon body // O' muscle of my timely end // if I had more in me, I would leave this thing here //   // the image that must cleave in its want // the weapon fully naked // in one lop, I would scissor off the part bit by the ill horse // in the house of no wave—in the breach // my hair is comely still, and made for a man's fist // the man knuckles a sea of feathers // gives to the fleshy knot // my bull-nuts // my loose scalp // when it is over, we do not tarry in our language // the quiet flings itself like a basehead // on my back, the memory is kept on a thread I pull to speak // that is an attempt to lose the man you know is everywhere // this is an attempt at a volta—two black boys chase each other through a hedgerow where no one can find // now neither one is it

Aidan Forster
Landscape with Horse & Two Boys Kissing

I held the wild hum of milk in my throat,
let my mouth become an artifact of light.

I blindfolded myself & named horses' bones
with my hands. I picked a boy from the fields

& we tumbled between the barn & the silo,
sold the bull of our kiss for a handful of seeds.

*

I know how to put my ugly things away:
how to hurl racehorses from their cells

when the bullet forgets itself. How to hold
my finger in the dip of the boy's ankle.

How to press a love note into his palm
in horsehair, body gone luster & limb.

*

We don't think of water until the creek
dries up. We don't think of our mothers

until after we fuck behind the barn:
how they kingdom the earth, white & bleak

like marigolds. We have nothing but a bridle
& the bucket we use to bob for apples.

Nathan Lipps
Foreign

This day.
Looking for the goat lost
over that hill. And finding
the gun.
Learning the music
of a spent cartridge.
And perfecting it.

There is no burial
for the body
without looking at the body.
We have abandoned the field
anyway, unwilling to dig.

There is only the brief pause of noon.
Shadowless. The smell of rust lifting
off the orchard floor.

Wind-knocked peaches feeding
the ancient grass bordering
every entryway, hungry.

A static hand upon your neck.
The miraculous erasure of home.
Catching your breath. Good
child. Good.
            Again.

Brennan Bestwick
Séance

A round of robins carries the drowned boys
up into the cedars. They drape their arms

over the branches and await morning.
At dawn, the birds split the boys' swollen

jaws. They lift their wet tongues and clean
bootlaces and silt from the boys' molars.

Fledglings squeeze down their throats
and descend into the ballooned lungs.

They reappear with knots of fishing line
and bottle caps pinched in their small beaks.

Single file, the robins follow each other out
of the boys, parting their pale blue lips.

The lake spills past the boys' chins and chests,
in their sneakers, to the roots of the trees.

The cedars rise. They lift the boys to the sun.
The boys blink. Each breathes again. They live.

Those of us who swam to boats that never sank
remember the weeks the helicopters circled.

The boys' families cried on television. We stayed
inside our homes. It became too easy to picture

our empty beds in the houses we grew up in.
We thought of our own parents' weeping on camera.

We prayed for those boys, to whatever we believed
God to be. We found birds, plump red breasted robins.

They followed us to school, slept on windowsills
outside the halls we lived between. We dreamed

of those boys breathing again, even after the divers
wouldn't scan the banks anymore and swimmers

stopped fearing every fin that grazed their feet.
The sky is a plea opposite drowning.

The birds bring the boys down from the trees,
three robins to a collar. The boys practice walking.

A heartbeat ripples through their wrists once more.
We watch the birds taxi each boy from the boughs

back to their feet. Those of us who have never died
don't dip our toes in the water anymore. We can't

leave the yard. We run from the sound of the tide
rolling in. The robins enclose us if we get too near water.

They push us towards the trees. Our safety belongs
to the woods, the trunk's long neck, wilderness.

When we hold our hands out to the birds they flutter
just beyond our reach. All the drowned boys laugh.

—Nominated by *Thrush Poetry Journal*

Adam J. Gellings
In Currents

We continue to receive bodies in currents along the shores
                        of the Rio Paraná   some days
they are scattered
   amongst the reeds   today   the curate helped identify the bodies
         found in the currents
but none were of the current mayor
                 the viejitos say the currents
have never had a diet

      a five-year-old was devoured like a redcurrant
              after the same current had bitten his parents
in Corrientes
      they picked up all the loose curs   & rent has gone up because
of the currency crisis
        the Chamamé festival was curtailed by bad
currents   at the present time
a warning is out
      for southern currents after a cavalcade of courier wagons
was lifted
like a bird's cry   when we go outside we feel the sky vibrate
                         with the probability
of currents
   inside before dark & close your curtains   but we still fish & piss
          & stand together in currents   no street
vendors have been arrested
        in currents for eleven days now   babies are born in
currents   disappear in currents   mothers
   read aloud the names of the disappeared

                                    as they march through the Plaza
                                        carrying photos of the missing
& signs written in cursive
pasted to the side of every current   when you turn a corner
                                            all you see
            are the curved faces & curled lips
of missing currents
        current after current   all mothers want answers   have you seen
my current they ask
& down with the currents they curse   it's all politics the viejitos say
                    but stay out of the way
of those swift moving currents.

Tyler Kline
What's Underneath Must Be Examined & Released

My lover holds me like a cat's glass eye. Insists
she can build a field out of the word *fireplace*

& she does: the trick is to let the words swallow each other
until neither of us can feel our phantom burns

& we are standing in snow, remembering the difference
between the joke that made the taxidermist laugh

& the one that made him cry. *Inside there is still a boy*
but tonight we have no way of knowing, tonight

our hands are pale horses distancing a burning barn
& they believe the hallelujah of bruise, of lips kissing

like birthday punches. We come alive as the liquor in us:
spoons of station-wagon smoke getting lost in guitars,

psalms ending in *eyelash* in *wet wood*. Downwind, you bury
my last dream: pajamas catching on the windowsill,

moon's teeth unable to free me when the rapture came.
On our knees we fall to earth like scythes returning

to dark rooms. In the end morning is just the time
we take to open the doe's mouth & find only snow.

Title after artist Sam Durant's project *Partially Buried / Altamont,* 1998

Madeleine Wattenberg
Ars Mythos

Like women, birds
                    are bad news.

They come with cutting
                    vanes and steel

rachis. Hercules
                    shot the Stymphalian,

but not before
                    they'd shed their swords

and wormed their beaks
                    into the farmers' lush

bodies. Here every
                    suffering will be made

visible or at least
                    not written out.

Consider how after
                    Procne's husband

rapes her sister,
                    she serves him their son's

flesh. One body
                entering another

in reprisal for the same.
                        All characters of this myth

live the remainder
                of their sufferings as birds.

Sister as nightingale—
                        symbol of scored

silence. The husband
                under the tarnished crown

of an orange crested
                hoopoe. Procne

transformed into a small
                        swallow, the act

of consumption. This punishment
                        requires she draw

into the cavity of her body
                        foreign pieces

of the world and let
                them live. I reject

that I can either consume
                        or want to be

consumed, but I
        admit I admire

the raptor that desires
        another's body

to keep beneath
        her glowing field
                of iron feathers.

Julia Kolchinsky Dasbach
Against Naming

Let's not name her or compare
flesh to fruit. Let's joke instead
how she swallowed a seed and let it
grow inside her. Just imagine,
how heavy is that sound and what
it tastes like in ripe summertime heat.
I had no cravings though. Only wanted to touch
the cold or be touched. Polish berries carried
the winter, so I ate them by the bucket.
Gooseberries, currants, sour cherries, bursting
childhood in my mouth. A past made sweeter
by its being passed. My mother sweating through
tolkuchka—the little push 'n' shove bazar—
to return home with a stained skirt and fruit
dangling from her ears and me, hungry
inside her. The Krakow market was a harvest too
this hottest July on record and in Oswiecim, the camps
didn't know what to do with all the people
in such heat, so at the gates of Auschwitz
sprinklers appeared—for the children mostly.
And you, my love, were just about the size
of an artichoke inside me then, its heart
soft and yours, wanting. Water and a past
that isn't this. One not passed down.
But I carried you there anyway. Against
my family's urges. Against even your future
ones, maybe. Walked you miles across
black ground turned red then gray then left

for colorless. The dead beneath us
silent. The ones around us, growing.
And I sang to you of a golden city
under a paling sky with its magic garden
and single star and the flame-maned lion
waiting there. You listened, my love, perhaps
they did too, ashes rising in the creek and in the petals,
Birkenau's waters and purple wildflowers,
its big book of names
from which we did not choose
to name you. Valen, valiant, strong, unmarked
by ancestry or first-generation or Slavic or fruit.
But V, for the survivor who refused
to be named that, for the numbered and unnumbered
names unwritten and scattered there, for the woman
who made seeds grow as gorgeous
out of flesh as out of stone.

M'Bilia Meekers
Hive

after Robin Coste Lewis

One morning I woke up wet and folded
in the center of a black gyre.

Sometimes, you'd speak from the outside,
or press your hand in the eye

to streak black specs against my cheek.
Other times, you'd release gold leaf

until the air swelled brighter than a singing beehive.
I told you, in SaLone my Aunt Shirley married a witch doctor

who fed her hallucinogenic tinctures by hand,
unsutured his voice

from the barrels of his throat and threw it at her.
Perhaps this is why

I looked you in the eye for too long,
wasn't watching

the way grains of sand began
to obscure your face

until even it became particulate.
When I said *schizophrenic*, you laughed, widened

your eye holes when I mouthed *ventriloquist*.
In the heart of the gyre, I found snakeskins and hands

severed in the 90s by the Revolutionary
United Front. You told me in every love story

there must be something keeping the couple split.
Bullshit I said and every so often I'd spin

songs above my head. I'd switch
from "Bloody Mary" to Billie Holiday in an instant

when I thought you weren't listening. And then,
Why are you so unhappy? you asked me. I could barely see

your silhouette, pitching rum and ganja
through the vortex. I buried them and hid

alligator gall between my breasts. I could leave
whenever I wanted, you said,

but soon I started finding pieces
of your face, revolving

everywhere I looked. A tooth. An iris.
A bottom lip. My name

came reeling towards me from a net
of insects that said it was your mouth.

There were so many, beating
blood through their wings, claiming

love, saying *drink this* to press
their stingers in my body.

—Nominated by *Guernica*

JD Scott
Altarpiece in Apricot Light

I took the Polaroid of my ex-boyfriend
down from the kitchen window sill.
It was sun-worn
as soon as the photo was taken. I mean,
it was an ancient pack of film I found
under a pile of junk that summer I moved
out of Brooklyn,
and he drove the U-Haul down
to Alabama with me, and the morning
before he flew back to the city
I watched him through that window,
snapped the shutter, the expired film coming
out as a ghost of rotten apricot,
and then I broke up with him
a few months later, because I've never
done well with the mathematics
of time + distance, and it's been two
years, this orange sherbert light bleached
thing of him on the green porch swing
that I shot from inside the house,
that I shot through glass and distance,
that I kept above the kitchen window so I could see
him while I did the dishes. The weird part is
I didn't even take the Polaroid
down because I wanted to get over him,
it's that the kitchen sink was clogged,
and I needed to let my landlady in

to take a look at the pipes,
and I was worried what she
would think, entering this old house,
finding my instant-film altar against the pane,
seeing his faded black bangs,
his white face looking out
at the street,
and her,
wondering what this photograph
could even mean to me.

Kara Krewer

Freeway

At night the driver in front
throws a cigarette out the window
and briefly, while it's still

glowing on the wind,
I want to swerve,

how the cherry looks like the shining eye
of an animal that didn't hear
us tearing down the road.

      I'm driving because
      I am always driving

now that I'm old enough. My mother nods off
under the prescription's haze, but she's here
      mumbling the song on the radio:

      I can't give you anything but…
      Nothing in this great big world but…

      Years from now
her car will be found in a ditch
beside the white stretch of cotton fields,

and she'll come to with a woman standing
over her shouting

She's dead!
She's dead!

     though she's not. My mother will say she swerved
as an animal crossed the freeway

but she can't keep it straight.
Raccoon one day, possum months later,
       sometimes a cat—

and she can tell me this again and again,
       grace being that an animal can change.

Roy G. Guzmán
Queerodactyl V

We'd begun vogueing in graveyards, headstones as big
      as Daddy's factory plant, *Playboy* magazines littered
under the bathroom sink, sour cream drip drops on our moustaches.
      No one knew whose mom had charred the tortillas.
We scraped marmoleum floors with our heels. Geometry
      went defunct, went apparel, berserk, bull in jeans, torero.
Our mothers neared their lips to our dirty claws
      as we swayed them in man's holy, unshaven catastrophes,
prayers so lit you'd think they went out to find a job. Because
      we no longer searched for food on the ground or in the sky
but knew border by its shame, plunged our bodies into it
      the way a father's hand might twist, tighten, rip a rosary.
Have we ever told you what else we felt when the earth's doors
      betrayed authority—when wind unfurled wig, crystal beads,
the sacrament in our hands? Had mercy shown up as mercy,
      we might have stopped the idealized throttle. Picked our hips
from the humid ground. Fashioned ourselves a new savior.

—Nominated by *The Collapsar*

Ösel Jessica Plante
Last December

I opened my life along its spine, a new blue emerged
two halves jolted apart like lips once frozen around
an ocean. Words can roll like peas from one side
of a plate to another like waves through a brain.
The skull begins soft, spoon-sized fontanelle, a new
blue in the brain. I once saw a human brain cut in two,
soft as pudding, grey as winter sea foam. God's voice
bursting as though from the long throats of cranes.
Here, at home, I've set my table, new plates, blue folded
cloth napkins to fly between my friends' laps and their
faces cut in two, as though touched by colored pencils.
Our tongues, our scars. We extend into one another
as if undressing in the shadows of a sycamore tree,
the plates of our faces erased. We stack each on each
our sable irises, our darkness, evening pressing us
as gentle as God's voice slipping upon the cosmos.
I strum along. He floats between me and what I mean
to be. On my knees, light goes everywhere I go. It's how
I know to praise the sycamore trees, a new blue, the ring
of light that goes where I go, arrives slow as bone.

Acknowledgments

Alfredo Aguilar's "On This Side of the Desert" previously appeared in *Winter Tangerine.*

Zaina Alsous's "Leave" previously appeared in The Asian American Writers' Workshop's *The Margins.*

Eloisa Amezcua's "Watching *Underworld, Inc.* Episode 3: 'Human Cargo'" previously appeared in *Public Poetry.*

Mary Angelino's "Unanswered Questions about the War" previously appeared in *Spillway.*

Brennan Bestwick's "Séance" previously appeared in *Thrush Poetry Journal.*

Kai Carlson-Wee's "Rail" previously appeared in *New England Review.*

Leila Chatti's "Motherland" previously appeared in *The Rumpus.*

Meghan Maguire Dahn's "Never Do Housework with Imperfect Intent" previously appeared in *Poetry Northwest.*

Bernard Ferguson's "On Eagerness" previously appeared in *Third Point Press.*

Jameson Fitzpatrick's "I Woke Up" previously appeared in *Poetry.*

Adam J. Gellings's "In Currents" previously appeared in *Prelude.*

Roy G. Guzmán's "Queerodactyl V" previously appeared in *The Collapsar*.

Christina Im's "Meanwhile in America" previously appeared in *The Adroit Journal*.

Tyler Kline's "What's Underneath Must Be Examined & Released" previously appeared in *Spoon River Poetry Review*.

Julia Kolchinsky Dasbach's "Against Naming" previously appeared in *New South*.

Kara Krewer's "Freeway" previously appeared in *Prairie Schooner*.

Edgar Kunz's "Free Armchair, Worcester" previously appeared in *Bat City Review*.

Kien Lam's "Ode to Working" previously appeared *Southern Indiana Review*.

K. T. Landon's "What We See, What Sees Us" previously appeared in *Breakwater Review*.

Paige Lewis's "The Moment I Saw a Pelican Devour" previously appeared in *Sixth Finch*.

Nathan Lipps's "Foreign" previously appeared in *Banango Street*.

Kristina Martino's "Kristina's World: After Wyeth" previously appeared in *Third Coast*.

M'Bilia Meekers's "Hive" previously appeared in *Guernica*.

Jonah Mixon Webster's "Excursus: A Reverie" previously appeared in
  Assaracus.

Vanessa Moody's "Anniversary III" previously appeared in
  Breakwater Review.

Xandria Phillips's "Social Death, an Address" previously appeared in
  Nashville Review.

Andres Rojas's "From the Lost Letters to Matias Perez, Aeronaut"
  previously appeared in *AGNI*.

Yuki Tanaka's "Death in Parentheses" previously appeared in *Poetry*.

Amanda Turner's "What Clowns" previously appeared in her chapbook
  Of Nectar, published by the Poetry Society of America.

Michael Wasson's "Self-Portrait as 1879–1934" previously appeared in
  Kenyon Review.

Madeleine Wattenberg's "Ars Mythos" previously appeared in
  Tinderbox Poetry Journal.

Keith S. Wilson's "God Particle" previously appeared in
  Crab Orchard Review.

Contributors' Notes

CHAD ABUSHANAB's poems appear in *Ecotone, Shenandoah, 32 Poems, Measure, The Hopkins Review,* and others. He is a PhD candidate in literature and creative writing at Texas Tech University. Find out more at chadabushanab.com.

ALFREDO AGUILAR is the son of Mexican immigrants. He is the author of the forthcoming chapbooks *Recuerdo* (YesYes Books, 2018) and *What Happens On Earth* (BOAAT Press 2018). He has received fellowships from VONA and the Bread Loaf Writers' Conference. His work has appeared or will soon appear in *The Adroit Journal, Muzzle, The Shallow Ends,* and elsewhere. He lives in North County San Diego.

ZAINA ALSOUS is a Palestinian writer and abolitionist, who was raised in North Carolina. Her poetry has appeared in *The Offing, Glass, decomP, Radius,* and elsewhere.

ELOISA AMEZCUA is an Arizona native. Her debut collection, *From the Inside Quietly,* is the inaugural winner of the Shelterbelt Poetry Prize selected by Ada Limón. She is the author of three chapbooks and is the founder and editor of *The Shallow Ends: A Journal of Poetry.* Her website is at eloisaamezcua.com.

MARY ANGELINO's recent publications include *Best New Poets 2015* and *2010, Spillway, PRISM international, Day One, Pleiades, New Ohio Review,* and *The Journal.* She teaches creative writing at College of the Canyons in Los Angeles, California.

FATIMAH ASGHAR is a member of the Dark Noise Collective, a Kundiman Fellow, a Fulbright Scholar, and a Ruth Lilly and Dorothy Sargent Rosenberg Fellow. She is the writer of *Brown Girls*, an Emmy-nominated web series. Her debut collection of poems, *If They Come for Us*, is forthcoming from One World, a Random House imprint. "How We Left: Film Treatment" won the Michael R Gutterman Award in Poetry from the University of Michigan.

SARAH HELEN BATES has an MFA in poetry from Northern Michigan University and teaches at Southern Utah University. Her work has appeared or is forthcoming in *American Literary Review, Seneca Review, The Normal School, Rattle, RHINO, Colorado Review,* and *Hotel Amerika,* among others.

BRYCE BERKOWITZ is an MFA candidate at West Virginia University. He is the editor-in-chief at *Cheat River Review*. His work has appeared or is forthcoming in *Third Coast, Passages North, The Pinch, Hobart, Barrow Street, Permafrost, Eleven Eleven, Tampa Review,* and *Hawai'i Pacific Review,* among other publications.

BRENNAN BESTWICK is a reader and writer from the Flint Hills of Kansas. His poems have been published in *Relief, Winter Tangerine, The Colorado Review,* and other journals. He is the winner of a AWP Intro Journals Project Award. His website is brennanbestwick.com.

KAI CARLSON-WEE is the author of *RAIL* (BOA Editions, 2018). His work has appeared in *Ploughshares, New England Review, Gulf Coast,* and *The Missouri Review,* which awarded him the 2013 Editor's Prize. His photography has been featured in *Narrative Magazine* and his poetry film, *Riding the Highline,* received jury awards at the 2015 Napa Valley Film Festival and the 2016 Arizona International Film Festival. A former Wallace Stegner Fellow, he lives in San Francisco and teaches poetry at Stanford University.

LEILA CHATTI is a Tunisian-American poet and author of the chapbooks *Ebb* (New-Generation African Poets Series) and *Tunsiya/Amrikiya*, the 2017 Editors' Selection from Bull City Press. She is the recipient of fellowships and awards from the Fine Arts Work Center in Provincetown, the Tin House Writer's Workshop, Dickinson House, the Barbara Deming Memorial Fund, and the Wisconsin Institute for Creative Writing, where she is the 2017–2018 Ron Wallace Poetry Fellow. Her poems have appeared in *Ploughshares*, *Tin House*, *The Georgia Review*, *Virginia Quarterly Review*, *New England Review*, *Narrative*, *The Rumpus*, and elsewhere.

MEGHAN MAGUIRE DAHN's work has appeared or is forthcoming in *Boston Review*, *The Iowa Review* online, *Cincinnati Review*, *Horsethief*, *Bennington Review*, *Blunderbuss*, *The Journal*, *Poetry Northwest*, *Phantom Limb*, and *Beloit Poetry Journal*, among others. She was a winner of the 92nd Street Y's 2014 Discovery Poetry Prize and holds an MFA from Columbia University's School of the Arts. She grew up in the woods and now lives steps from Manhattan's only forest.

JULIA KOLCHINSKY DASBACH emigrated from Dnepropetrovsk, Ukraine, as a Jewish refugee when she was six years old. She holds an MFA in poetry from the University of Oregon and is a PhD candidate in comparative literature at the University of Pennsylvania where her research focuses on contemporary American poetry about the Holocaust. She has received fellowships from the Bread Loaf and TENT Conferences as well as the Auschwitz Jewish Center. Julia is the author of *The Bear Who Ate the Stars* (Split Lip Press, 2014) and her poems have appeared in *Gulf Coast*, *TriQuarterly*, and *Beloit Poetry Journal*, among others. Julia is editor of *Construction Magazine* and writes a blog about motherhood at otherwomendonttellyou.wordpress.com.

SAMANTHA DEAL's poetry and nonfiction have appeared or are forthcoming in *Quarterly West*, *Hunger Mountain*, *Word Riot*, *The Boiler*,

Sonora Review, Tupelo Quarterly, Rattle, Ninth Letter, The Journal, and others. She has been a finalist for the Zone 3 First Book Award, the Mississippi Review Poetry Prize, the OSU Press/The Journal Wheeler Prize, the Saturnalia Books Poetry Prize, and the American Literary Review's Poetry Prize, among others. Her debut collection, *[Something Opened],* is forthcoming from Black Lawrence Press. She lives and works in Kalamazoo, Michigan, where she is a doctoral candidate at Western Michigan University. You can keep up with her at samanthaldeal.com.

BERNARD FERGUSON is a Bahamian immigrant trying to plant his feet in Minnesota. He has work featured or upcoming in *Epiphany Magazine, FreezeRay Poetry, Mizna, The Santa Ana River Review,* and *Tinderbox Poetry Journal,* among others. He has a website at bernardferguson.com. He wants you to tell him about the last film that made you cry.

JAMESON FITZPATRICK's poems have appeared or are forthcoming in *The American Poetry Review, Poetry, The New Yorker,* and elsewhere. He lives in New York, where he teaches at New York University.

AIDAN FORSTER is a senior in high school studying creative writing at the South Carolina Governor's School for the Arts and Humanities in Greenville, South Carolina. His work appears in *BOAAT, Cimarron Review, Indiana Review, Pleiades, Muzzle, Sixth Finch,* and *Verse,* among others. His debut chapbook of poems, *Exit Pastoral,* was a finalist for the 2017 Vinyl 45s Chapbook Contest and is forthcoming from YesYes Books in 2018.

M.K. FOSTER is a poet and renaissance literature scholar from Birmingham, Alabama. Her poetry has appeared or is forthcoming in *The Columbia Review, Crazyhorse, Rattle, The Adroit Journal, Sixth Finch, B O D Y, New Orleans Review, Ninth Letter,* and elsewhere, and her work has been recognized with a *Gulf Coast Poetry Prize,* an Academy of American Poets Prize, two Pushcart Prize nominations, and a *Best of the Net* nomination.

She holds an MFA from the University of Maryland and is currently pursuing a PhD at the University of Alabama. Additional notes and links can be found through her website at marykatherinefoster.com.

ADAM J. GELLINGS is a poet from Columbus, Ohio.

SAMANTHA GRENROCK grew up in California. She received an MFA from the University of Florida and is the 2017 winner of the *Cincinnati Review's* Robert and Adele Schiff Award in Poetry. Her work has appeared or is forthcoming in *New Orleans Review, Horsethief, Raritan*, and others. "It Is Known to the State of California" is part of a manuscript-in-progress on how to feel and think about climate change and ecological crisis.

ROY G. GUZMÁN was born in Honduras and raised in Miami, Florida. He is a 2017 Ruth Lilly and Dorothy Sargent Rosenberg Poetry Fellow and a Minnesota State Arts Board Initiative grant recipient. His work has appeared in *Poetry, Meridian, Juked, Jet Fuel Review*, and *Winter Tangerine*. His website is at roygguzman.com.

CHRISTINA IM is a Korean-American writer and high school student from Portland, Oregon. A *Best of the Net* nominee, she has been recognized for her writing by Princeton University, Bennington College, Hollins University, and the National YoungArts Foundation. Her work appears in *The Adroit Journal, The Blueshift Journal*, and *Wildness*, among others.

Ben Kingsley is best known for his Academy Award winning role as Mahatma Gandhi. A touch less famous, BENJAMÍN NAKA-HASEBE KINGSLEY has not acted since his third-grade debut as the undertaker in *Music Man*. A Kundiman and UPenn alumni, Ben is the twenty-second Tickner Writing Fellow and recipient of a Provincetown Fine Arts Work Center fellowship as well as scholarships from Sewanee and VONA. He belongs to the Onondaga Nation of Indigenous Americans in New

York. His work can be found in the *Iowa Review, Narrative, Ninth Letter, PANK, PEN America, The Poetry Review, Prairie Schooner*, and *Tin House*, among others.

TYLER KLINE is the author of the chapbook *As Men Do Around Knives* (ELJ Editions, 2016). Currently, he teaches in Pennsylvania and works on an organic herb farm. He was named poet laureate of Bucks County in 2015. Visit him online at tylerklinepoetry.com.

KARA KREWER grew up on an orchard in rural Georgia. Her poems have appeared in *The Georgia Review, Prairie Schooner, The Adroit Journal, Ninth Letter*, and elsewhere. She holds an MFA in poetry from Purdue University, and is a 2016–2018 Stegner Fellow at Stanford University.

EDGAR KUNZ is from Massachusetts. A 2017 National Endowment for the Arts Fellow and former Wallace Stegner Fellow at Stanford, his first book, *TAP OUT*, is forthcoming from Houghton Mifflin Harcourt/ Mariner in 2019. He lives in Oakland, California.

SHANE LAKE is the author of *The Bone Trees*, a digital chapbook available from BOAAT Press. His poems have appeared in *Beloit Poetry Journal, New Ohio Review, Indiana Review, Narrative, Third Coast*, and elsewhere. He lives and teaches in Oklahoma City.

KIEN LAM is a Kundiman Fellow and received an MFA in poetry from Indiana University. His poetry has appeared or is forthcoming from *The Nation, Kenyon Review, Ploughshares*, and elsewhere. He currently lives in Los Angeles, where he writes about eSports. Follow him on Twitter @meanmisterkien.

K. T. LANDON is the author of the chapbook *Orange, Dreaming* (Five Oaks Press, 2017). She received her MFA from Vermont College of Fine Arts and her work has been nominated for the Pushcart Prize and the *Best of the Net* anthology. She serves as a reader for *Muzzle* and her poems have appeared or are forthcoming in *Narrative, New Millennium Writings,* and *Passages North,* among others. Find her online at ktlandon.com. "What We See, What Sees Us" is for Bud Tibbetts.

PAIGE LEWIS is the author of the chapbook *Reasons to Wake You* (Tupelo Press, 2018). Their poems have appeared or are forthcoming in *American Poetry Review, Ploughshares, The Georgia Review,* and elsewhere.

NATHAN LIPPS's work has appeared or is forthcoming in *Typo, Third Coast, The Colorado Review, Banango Street, BOAAT, Tammy,* and elsewhere. He currently studies and works in central New York state.

KRISTINA MARTINO is a poet and visual artist. Her poems have appeared in *BOAAT, Third Coast, Bennington Review, Bateau,* and elsewhere. She attended the Iowa Writers' Workshop and the Pennsylvania Academy of the Fine Arts, and is a forthcoming Wolff Cottage Writer-in-Residence at the Fairhope Center for the Writing Arts. For more, see kristinamartino.com.

ERIN L. McCOY holds an MFA in poetry and an MA in Hispanic studies from the University of Washington. Her poetry has been published or is forthcoming in *Bennington Review, Pleiades, DIAGRAM, The Tusculum Review, CURA,* and other publications. She is the public relations manager for Open Books, Seattle's poetry-only bookstore, and is a recipient of numerous awards, including a Fulbright Fellowship, the University of Washington's Grace Milliman Pollock Scholarship, and the Oakley Hall III Memorial Scholarship to attend the Community of Writers in Squaw Valley, California. She is from Louisville, Kentucky. Her website is erinlmccoy.com.

M'BILIA MEEKERS was raised in New Orleans, Louisiana, with roots in Belgium and Sierra Leone. She is the author of a chapbook, *Wish for a Drowned Daughter,* and has received fellowships from Poets & Writers, Cave Canem, and The Watering Hole. She is the winner of Tulane University's Academy of American Poets Prize (2015) and the Marble Faun Poetry Award (2011), among other honors. Her work has previously appeared or is forthcoming in *The New Yorker, Guernica, Poet Lore, Tinderbox, Calamity, Wildness, Tulane Review* and other publications. She received her bachelor's in English literature from Tulane University in 2015 and her MFA in creative writing from NYU in 2017.

JONAH MIXON-WEBSTER is a poet, sound artist, and educator from Flint, Michigan. He is the author of *Stereo(TYPE)* (2018 Ahsahta Press), and is a PhD candidate in English studies at Illinois State University. His poetry and hybrid works are featured or forthcoming in *Callaloo, Barzakh Journal, Spoon River Poetry Review, Assaracus,* LA Review of Books' *Voluble,* and *Best American Experimental Writing 2018.* Along with Casey Rocheteau, he is a founding member of the multidisciplinary black arts collective CTTNN Club (Can't Take These Niggas Nowhere).

VANESSA MOODY is a Brazilian-American writer and artist living in New York. Her work appears in online and print publications, including *Willow Springs* and *Breakwater Review.* Also a librettist, Vanessa's opera *What Gets Kept* premiered at the Kennedy Center. She earned her BA in English at Stanford University and her MFA in poetry at NYU, where she was a Goldwater Fellow and undergraduate instructor. Vanessa works in children's publishing and is a proud Hufflepuff.

ANNA NEWMAN's work has appeared in *Third Coast, Houseguest, Crab Fat,* and other journals. She is currently completing her MFA in poetry at the University of Maryland, where she teaches freshman composition and creative writing.

ALYSSA OGI is a writer and teacher in Portland, Oregon. She received her MFA from the University of Oregon, and her poetry can be found in *The Crab Orchard Review, burntdistrict,* and other journals.

XANDRIA PHILLIPS is the author of *Reasons for Smoking*, which won the 2016 *Seattle Review* chapbook contest judged by Claudia Rankine. Xandria is the poetry editor at Honeysuckle Press, the associate poetry editor for *Winter Tangerine*, and the curator of *Love Letters to Spooks*. She has received fellowships from Cave Canem and Callaloo. Her poetry has appeared or is forthcoming in *Beloit Poetry Journal*, *Bettering American Poetry*, the *Shade Journal*, *The Journal*, *The Offing*, and elsewhere. Find her at xandriaphillips.com.

ÖSEL JESSICA PLANTE's poetry, and flash fiction, has appeared or is forthcoming in the *Best Small Fictions 2016* anthology, *The Adroit Journal*, *Puerto del Sol*, *South Dakota Review*, the *minnesota review*, *Mid-American Review*, *Mississippi Review*, *New Ohio Review*, *Rattle*, *Zone 3*, and others. She was runner-up in *Meridian*'s 2017 poetry contest and a finalist for the 2016 Mississippi Review Prize. She earned an MFA from UNC-Greensboro and is pursuing a PhD in poetry at Florida State University. More of her work can be found at oseljessicaplante.com.

CAITLIN ROACH received an MFA in poetry from the Iowa Writers' Workshop, where she was a Provost Fellow and the recipient of a Post-Graduate Fellowship. Her work has appeared or is forthcoming in *Poetry Northwest*, *Colorado Review*, *Copper Nickel*, *West Branch*, *Prelude*, *Handsome*, and *The Iowa Review*. She teaches creative writing and literature at the University of Nevada, Las Vegas, where she is an assistant professor-in-residence. More of her work can be found at caitlinroach.com.

ANDRÉS ROJAS was born in Cuba and came to the United States at age thirteen. He holds an MFA from the University of Florida and is the author of the audio chapbook *The Season of the Dead* (EAT Poems, 2016). His poems have most recently appeared or are forthcoming in *AGNI*, *Barrow Street*, *Colorado Review*, *Massachusetts Review*, *Mid-American Review*, *New England Review*, *New American Writing*, *Notre Dame Review*, and *Poetry Northwest*, among others.

JD Scott is a writer, poet, and editor. Recent and forthcoming publications include *Best American Experimental Writing, Denver Quarterly, Prairie Schooner, Salt Hill, Sonora Review, Ninth Letter, Tampa Review,* and elsewhere. More of JD can be found at jdscott.com.

YUKI TANAKA was born and raised in Yamaguchi, Japan, and is currently an MFA student at the Michener Center for Writers at the University of Texas–Austin. His poems have appeared in the *Denver Quarterly, The Margins, Poetry,* and *West Branch*. His translations of modern Japanese poetry (with Mary Jo Bang) have appeared in *New Republic, Kenyon Review, Paris Review,* and *A Public Space,* among other journals. He also serves as poetry editor of *Bat City Review*.

AMANDA TURNER is the author of the chapbook *Of Nectar,* selected and introduced by A. Van Jordan for the 2015 Poetry Society of America Chapbook Fellowship, where "What Clowns" originally appeared. A graduate of Columbia University's School of the Arts, she has taught poetry writing and composition at Santa Clara University and has served as an assistant poetry editor for *Poetry Northwest*. Her poems have appeared in *Calyx, The Western Humanities Review, COLUMBIA: A Journal of Literature and Art, The Sycamore Review, Fourteen Hills,* and other publications. She lives in Portland, Oregon, with her husband and daughter.

MICHAEL WASSON's poems appear in *American Poets, Beloit Poetry Journal, Drunken Boat, Gulf Coast, Poetry Northwest, Narrative,* and *Bettering American Poetry*. He is Nimíipuu from the Nez Perce Reservation in Idaho.

MADELEINE WATTENBERG's work has recently appeared or is forthcoming in journals such as *Fairy Tale Review, Tupelo Quarterly, Mid-American Review, Ninth Letter,* and *Guernica*. She received her MFA from George Mason University and is currently a PhD student in poetry at the University of Cincinnati.

KEITH S. WILSON is an Affrilachian poet, Cave Canem fellow, and graduate of the Callaloo Creative Writing Workshop. He has received scholarships from Bread Loaf, MacDowell, UCross, and Millay Colony. Keith serves as assistant poetry editor at *Four Way Review* and digital media editor at *Obsidian Journal*.

CONNOR YECK's poems have appeared or are forthcoming in *Crab Orchard Review, Southern Poetry Review,* and *Exceptions,* among others. He is currently an MFA student at Western Michigan University.

LILY ZHOU is a high school senior from the San Francisco Bay Area. Her work appears in *Sixth Finch, The Adroit Journal, SOFTBLOW,* and on *Verse Daily.*

Participating Magazines

32 Poems
32poems.com

The Account
theaccountmagazine.com

The Adroit Journal
theadroitjournal.org

AGNI Magazine
bu.edu/agni

Alligator Juniper
alligatorjuniper.org

The Antioch Review
review.antiochcollege.edu

Apple Valley Review
applevalleyreview.com

apt
apt.aforementionedproductions
.com

ARTS & LETTERS
artsandletters.gcsu.edu

Atlanta Review
atlantareview.com

Atticus Review
atticusreview.org

Barrelhouse
barrelhousemag.com

Bellingham Review
bhreview.org

Beloit Poetry Journal
bpj.org

Birmingham Poetry Review
uab.edu/cas/englishpublications/
birmingham-poetry-review

The Bitter Oleander
bitteroleander.com

Blood Orange Review
bloodorangereview.com

The Boiler Journal
theboilerjournal.com

The Bookends Review
thebookendsreview.com

Boulevard
boulevardmagazine.org

Boxcar Poetry Review
boxcarpoetry.com

Brick
brickmag.com

cahoodaloodaling
cahoodaloodaling.com

The Carolina Quarterly
thecarolinaquarterly.com

Carve Magazine
carvezine.com

Cincinnati Review
cincinnatireview.com

The Collagist
thecollagist.com

The Collapsar
thecollapsar.com

concīs
concis.io

Copper Nickel
copper-nickel.org

The Cossack Review
thecossackreview.com

Crab Fat Magazine
crabfatmagazine.com

Crazyhorse
english.cofc.edu/graduate-
    programs/master-fine-arts-
    creative-writing

Cumberland River Review
crr.trevecca.edu

Cutthroat
cutthroatmag.com

Ecotone
ecotonemagazine.org

EVENT Magazine
eventmagazine.ca

Fjords Review
fjordsreview.com

Foglifter
foglifterpress.com

Foothill: A Journal of Poetry
cgu.edu/foothill

Foundry
foundryjournal.com

The Fourth River
thefourthriver.com

Free State Review
freestatereview.com

The Georgia Review
thegeorgiareview.com

Gettysburg Review
gettysburgreview.com

Gingerbread House
gingerbreadhouselitmag.com

Glass: A Journal of Poetry
glass-poetry.com/journal.html

Golden Walkman Magazine
goldwalkmag.com

Greensboro Review
greensbororeview.org

Grist: A Journal of the Literary Arts
gristjournal.com

Guernica
guernicamag.com

Gulf Coast
gulfcoastmag.org

Hamilton Arts & Letters
HALmagazine.com

Harvard Review
harvardreview.org

Hermeneutic Chaos Literary Journal
hermeneuticchaosjournal.com

Hot Metal Bridge
hotmetalbridge.org

After Happy Hour Review
afterhappyhourreview.com

Image
imagejournal.org

IthacaLit
ithacalit.com

Jabberwock Review
jabberwock.org.msstate.edu

The Journal
english.osu.edu/mfa

Juked
juked.com

The Lascaux Review
lascauxreview.com

Lunch Ticket
lunchticket.org

The MacGuffin
schoolcraft.edu/macguffin

Malahat Review
malahatreview.ca

Massachusetts Review
massreview.org

Memorious: A Journal of New Verse & Fiction
memorious.org

Mid-American Review
casit.bgsu.edu/midamericanreview

The Minnesota Review
minnesotareview.dukejournals.org

Muzzle Magazine
muzzlemagazine.com

The Nashville Review
as.vanderbilt.edu/nashvillereview

Naugatuck River Review
naugatuckriverreview.com

New England Review
nereview.com

New Ohio Review
ohio.edu/nor

Nimrod International Journal
utulsa.edu/nimrod

Ninth Letter
ninthletter.com

Pacifica Literary Review
pacificareview.com

PANK
pankmagazine.com

Passages North
passagesnorth.com

Pembroke Magazine
pembrokemagazine.com

Phoebe
phoebejournal.com

Pittsburgh Poetry Review
pittsburghpoetryreview.com

Ploughshares
pshares.org

The Pinch
pinchjournal.com

Poetry
poetrymagazine.org

The Poet's Billow
thepoetsbillow.org

Pretty Owl Poetry
prettyowlpoetry.com

Puerto del Sol
puertodelsol.org

Quarterly West
quarterlywest.com

Radar Poetry
radarpoetry.com

Raleigh Review
RaleighReview.org

Rat's Ass Review
ratsassreview.net

Rattle
rattle.com

Reservoir
reservoirlit.com

River Styx
riverstyx.org

Roanoke Review
roanokereview.org

Ruminate Magazine
ruminatemagazine.com

Rush
therushmag.com

Sequestrum
sequestrum.org

The Shallow Ends
theshallowends.com

Slippery Elm
slipperyelm.findlay.edu

Smartish Pace
smartishpace.com

The Southeast Review
southeastreview.org

Southern Indiana Review
usi.edu/sir

The Southern Review
thesouthernreview.org

Spillway
spillway.org

storySouth
storysouth.com

Sugar House Review
SugarHouseReview.com

Sundog
sundoglit.com

Sycamore Review
sycamorereview.com

Tahoma Literary Review
tahomaliteraryreview.com

Third Coast
thirdcoastmagazine.com

Thrush Poetry Journal
thrushpoetryjournal.com

Tinderbox Poetry Journal
tinderboxpoetry.com

The Tishman Review
thetishmanreview.com

TRACK//FOUR
trackfourjournal.com

Tupelo Quarterly
tupeloquarterly.com

upstreet
upstreet-mag.org

Up the Staircase Quarterly
upthestaircase.org

Virginia Quarterly Review
vqronline.org

Washington Square Review
washingtonsquarereview.com

Waxwing Literary Journal
waxwingmag.org

Whale Road Review
whaleroadreview.com

wildness
readwildness.com

Yemassee
yemasseejournal.com

Participating Programs

American University Creative Writing Program
american.edu/cas/literature/mfa

Antioch University Los Angeles Low-Residency MFA
antioch.edu/los-angeles/degrees-programs/
    creative-writing-communication-studies/creative-writing-mfa

College of Charleson MFA in Creative Writing
english.cofc.edu/graduate-programs/master-fine-arts-creative-writing

Florida International University MFA in Creative Writing
english.fiu.edu/creative-writing

Florida State University Creative Writing
english.fsu.edu/programs/creative-writing

George Mason University MFA in Creative Writing
creativewriting.gmu.edu

Hollins University Jackson Center for Creative Writing
hollinsmfa.wordpress.com

Institute of American Indian Arts MFA in Creative Writing
mfa.iaia.edu

Kansas State University MFA in Creative Wriiting Program
k-state.edu/english/programs/cw

McNeese State University MFA Program
mfa.mcneese.edu

Minnesota State University Mankato Creative Writing Program
english.mnsu.edu/cw/index.html

Mount Saint Mary's University MFA in Creative Writing
msmu.edu/creativewriting

New Mexico Highlands University MA in English (Creative Writing)
nmhu.edu/current-students/graduate/arts-and-sciences/english

New Mexico State University MFA in Creative Wriiting
english.nmsu.edu/graduate-programs/mfa

New School Writing Program
newschool.edu/writing

New York University Creative Writing Program
cwp.as.nyu.edu

North Carolina State Creative Writing
english.chass.ncsu.edu/graduate/mfa

Northwestern University MA/MFA in Creative Writing
sps.northwestern.edu/program-areas/graduate/creative-writing

The Ohio State University MFA Program
english.osu.edu/mfa

Ohio University Creative Writing PhD
ohio.edu/cas/english/grad/creative-writing/index.cfm

Pacific University Master of Fine Arts in Writing
pacificu.edu/as/mfa

Sarah Lawrence College MFA in Writing
sarahlawrence.edu/writing-mfa

Southeast Missouri State University Master of Arts in English
semo.edu/english

Syracuse University MFA in Creative Writing
english.syr.edu/cw/cw-program.html

Texas Tech University Creative Writing Program
depts.ttu.edu/english/cw

UMass Amherst MFA for Poets and Writers
umass.edu/englishmfa

UMass Boston MFA Program in Creative Writing
umb.edu/academics/cla/english/grad/mfa

University of Alabama at Birmingham Graduate Theme in Creative Writing
uab.edu/cas/english/graduate-program/creative-writing

University of British Columbia Creative Writing Program
creativewriting.ubc.ca

University of Connecticut Creative Writing Program
creativewriting.uconn.edu

University of Illinois at Chicago Program for Writers
engl.uic.edu/CW

University of Illinois MFA in Creative Writing
creativewriting.english.illinois.edu

University of Kansas Graduate Program in Creative Writing
englishcw.ku.edu

University of Maryland MFA Program
english.umd.edu

University of Memphis MFA in Creative Wriiting
memphis.edu/english/graduate/mfa/creative_writing.php

University of Michigan Helen Zell Writers' Program
lsa.umich.edu/writers

University of Mississippi MFA in Creative Writing
mfaenglish.olemiss.edu

University of Missouri Creative Writing
english.missouri.edu/areas-study?q=area/creative-writing

University of North Texas Creative Writing
english.unt.edu/creative-writing-0

University of Notre Dame Creative Writing Program
english.nd.edu/creative-writing

University of Texas Michener Center for Writers
michener.utexas.edu

University of Utah Creative Writing MFA
english.utah.edu

Vermont College of Fine Arts MFA in Writing
vcfa.edu

Virginia Tech MFA in Creative Wriiting Program
liberalarts.vt.edu/academics/graduate-programs/masters-programs-list/
 master-of-fine-arts-in-creative-writing.html

Western Michigan University Master of Fine Arts in Creative Writing
wmich.edu/english

West Virginia University MFA Program
creativewriting.wvu.edu

The series editor wishes to thank the many readers involved in selecting the first round of finalists:

Sara Brickman, Michaela Cowgill, Michael Dhyne, Caitlin Fitzpatrick, Courtney Flerlage, Quinn Gilman-Forlini, Landis Grenville, Nichole LeFebvre, Sasha Prevost, Rob Shapiro, and Anna Tomlinson.

Special thanks to Jason Coleman and the University of Virginia Press for editorial advice and support.